Praise for *The Abol*

'The most sustained, internally logical and
powerful attack on Tony Blair and all his works'
Andrew Marr, *The Observer*

'Politically important'
Will Hutton

'a cri de coeur from an honest, intelligent and
patriotic Englishman, desperately worried
about the corruption of his country and the
likely effects of its lurch into the embraces
of a European superstate'
Tom Utley, *Daily Telegraph*

'A very useful book... Mad, obnoxious, elegantly
written... it draws up the true battle lines of
politics now far better than many of the
attempts to summarize the slippery Third Way
or the heart of Blairism'
Polly Toynbee, *The Guardian*

'I picked up Peter Hitchen's book with
apprehension... three and a half hours later
I put it down exhilarated. He has written
with passion and flair...'
John Redwood, *The Spectator*

By the same author and published by Quartet Books

The Abolition of Britain

Peter Hitchens

Monday Morning Blues

Quartet Books

DAILY EXPRESS

Published in Great Britain by Quartet Books Limited
A member of the Namara Group
27 Goodge Street
London W1P 2LD

A catalogue record for this book is available from the British Library

ISBN 0 7043 8156 7

Phototypeset by FiSH Books, London
Printed and bound in Great Britain by Cox & Wyman, Reading, Berks

Contents

Preface   vii
Crime   1
The Euro Rouble   15
Culture/Morals   31
Drugs   69
Sexism   77
Kosovo   89
History   97
Monarchy   100
Education   110
Liberty   119
Ulster   126
Foreign Affairs and Politics   135
Blairs   164
BBC   178
Human Rights   188
Soft on Communism   191
Miscellaneous   194
Lords   215

Preface

In this small book, I have tried to collect the articles and columns tht I am most pleased to have written for the *Daily Express*. Some, like the account of an execution which opens the selection, date from long before I began a regular column more than three years ago, but I think they form part of ther story I have tried to tell.

I hope that some of these words have given pleasure, comfort or encouragement to the many who share my opinions and who have been kind enough to write, telephone and e-mail to say so. Perhaps, gathered in a more permanent form, they will continue to do so.

Peter Hitchens
Oxford
October 2000

CRIME

Spitting killer goes to electric chair and the *Express* is the only British newspaper there

Nicholas Lee Ingram spat in the face of death, too angry over his fate to be afraid of the terrifying process he was about to undergo. It was a strange, sad and pointless courage – and I will always wish that he had used his last moments to admit his crime and offer some sort of apology to those whose lives he ruined when he murdered J. C. Sawyer almost 12 years ago.

For here in Jackson, Georgia, I was watching the deliberate death of a human being, powerful, solemn and violent. And that human being, for all he or I knew, was right at the mouth of hell with one last chance of redemption.

This was not the random tragedy of a road accident, the listless despair of an African child caught in a famine nor the savage slaughter of a defenceless civilian cut down by Soviet troops. I have seen these, and they are quite different.

When 2,000 volts surged into Nicholas Lee Ingram, it was by the cold, implacable decision of the people of the State of Georgia. When his cowled tightly-strapped body jerked in its bonds, so hard that I could hear it smack against the polished back of the electric chair, it was with the permission of the United States Supreme Court.

By chance, and just minutes before I was due to be taken to Georgia's death house, I was shown photographs of the body of J. C. Sawyer after Ingram had finished with him.

Lashed pitilessly to a tree, taunted, beaten before the eyes of his terrified wife, Mr Sawyer died a death far more grisly than the electric chair. No appeals for him, no British lawyer to sob as he passed away, no Archbishop of Canterbury to plead for his life.

It was necessary to remember those photographs as I was driven in a barred prison van, through the sweet smelling pine woods, to death row itself.

A vast peach-coloured sunset was fading to darkness, the last sunset Nicholas Ingram would see.

The prison, like all such places, was designed to make the soul sink – a structure like a nuclear bunker, hidden from the outside world by great banks of earth reached through a long underground tunnel.

Searched and checked, I was driven through razor-wire fences to the anonymous concrete building where Georgia's electric chair sits.

The first shock was the big green generator parked just outside, ready to roar into action and provide the deadly current.

But that was nothing compared to the impact of walking into the death chamber itself . . .

Three wooden church pews, face a window which stretches the width of the room – about 18ft.

Beyond the window sits the so far empty chair, a square, ugly, uncomfortable-looking throne of polished pine, with a headpiece and a huge array of well-worn brown leather straps and buckles.

The breezeblock walls are painted cream.

Two blood-red doors lead to mysterious regions beyond – the death cell where Ingram is waiting, and the control room where three executioners wait to press their fatal buttons.

Only one of them will actually begin the computerised process, and nobody will ever know which it is.

A one-way mirror conceals the executioners from sight Somewhere in the background, an official is on the phone to Washington DC, getting confirmation from Justice Anthony Kennedy of the Supreme Court that the execution can go ahead.

It can. Warden Jerry Thomas steps into the room and reads the formal announcement: "We will proceed with the court-ordered execution."

The witness room is full. The officers who arrested Ingram

and the man who prosecuted him, Georgia Attorney General Michael Bowers, sit on the pews or stand around the edge of the room in stiff, solemn silence.

Alone among this cloud of hostile witnesses is Clive Stafford Smith, Ingram's clever and determined British lawyer. He is witnessing the results of his failure.

Suddenly the other side of the room is full, too. Ingram appears, surrounded by six hefty warders. Their burly shapes and blue uniforms almost blot out Ingram's slight and wiry form.

The condemned man's face is almost rigid with tension. His head, newly shaved, is stark white, even whiter than his freshly-pressed and laundered uniform, with its strangely jaunty blue trim. They have left his straggly Viking moustache unshaved.

Hands and feet free for the last time in his life, Ingram walks unaided to the chair, sits down and even slides himself back on its hard pine seat, as if his comfort matters at such a moment. A tattoo on his left arm, crucial in his identification as a murderer, is clearly visible. It says Nick.

All the time he glares in the general direction of the witnesses. Everyone is trying to avoid catching his eye, except for Stafford Smith. He tries and fails to offer his client a last reassuring view of a friendly face.

Ingram's furious, resentful glare is for everyone. His face has grown hollow in prison and his eyes are extraordinarily deep-set.

The warders bend attentively round him, securing the heavy straps as tight as they will go, at ankles, thighs, waist, wrists and chest. It seems to take minutes to get them all secured but it is probably much quicker.

This has been rehearsed – using a volunteer roughly Ingram's size – many times in the past week.

I have been expecting trouble at this point since I saw Ingram in his final court appearance on Wednesday. Chained, shackled and manacled, he had looked ready to explode with fury, rocking back and forth in his bonds.

Now the warden asks him: "Do you have anything you would like to add to your final statement?"

(That "final statement", given the day before, consisted of the words "I have nothing to say to you or your tape recorder", delivered in such a menacing manner that the official involved was thoroughly scared.)

Incredibly, Ingram moves his head towards the warder and spits a great glob of saliva across the room with all the force he can muster. It misses.

Unmoved, the warden asks: "Would you like to have a prayer offered?"

Ingram closes his eyes. Death is very close. The warders advance again and fasten one more strap, a thick chin-piece which prevents Ingram's mouth from opening. He stares out, pathetic now, a trussed, muzzled creature without the power to move or speak.

Warders produce a headpiece rather like an old-fashioned rugby scrum-cap. In it is a sort of sponge, containing fluid which will ease the flow of power.

They bring up the cable from behind and secure it to the cap with a wing-nut. The other cable is connected to his right leg. A warder wipes Ingram's face with a towel.

Ingram is still staring and glowering when – and it is a mercy – they produce the cowl, a smooth sheet of brown leather which clips to the headpiece and covers his face, falling to his chest. It is 9.05 pm local time, 2.05 am in London, five minutes later than the appointed hour; Ingram's fists, clenched tight, are our only clue to his state of mind.

The officials withdraw.

Then, with the sudden force of a fist in the face, the power is switched on. Ingram jerks backwards with such violence that his body thwacks against the back of the chair. His fists clench still tighter, so that the knuckles are almost blue.

Experts believe – and hope – that this first shock has stunned him and that he is not now in pain. There is no way of telling. He does *not* writhe. There is neither smoke nor flame nor sizzling nor sparks.

As the voltage drops from 2,000 to 1,000 to 200, his fists

unclench slightly.

Mr Stafford Smith, who has held his hands in front of his eyes – except for one small peep through his fingers – is now weeping silently.

After seven or eight minutes, the warden and two doctors appear. The medics open Ingram's shirt and apply stethoscopes. They mouth something to the warden.

He steps forwards to announce: "At approximately 9.15 pm on April 7th, the court-ordered execution was carried out in accordance with the laws of the State of Georgia."

Later, a prison official will tell me that the only marks on the body are blisters where the electrodes touched. She will also assure me that Ingram's eyes most certainly did not pop out of their sockets, as many protesters believe.

Curtains are drawn across the windows and we are hurried out of the room. As I leave, the generator is winding down and a low, black hearse is creeping past the razor-wire to collect the body.

Nicholas Ingram, who told his victims "I like to torture people", and has never really admitted his crime, has gone to his final appeal.

9/4/95

An Arab knows crimes are punished and wrong avenged

How dare we sneer at Saudi Arabia's ferocious treatment of offenders? Their methods have many faults, it is true, but is our miserable failure of a justice system really so good that we can look down on them?

We may be very nice to offenders but how does our behaviour towards victims look to an Arab, who at least knows that crimes are punished and wrong is avenged?

In Britain, those who undergo robbery or violence are left to suffer, while the thieves and brutes who caused them pain are let off – that's if they are ever caught in the first place.

Here, serious criminal cases are routinely dropped because prosecutors cannot be bothered to fight them.

Yet a lawyer who defends crooks can become very rich indeed, while a prosecutor will usually stay poor. The best talent, naturally, goes into defence.

In "civilised" Britain, killers often go to jail for just four or five years because it is easier, cheaper and quicker for the system to accept a plea of guilty to manslaughter rather than murder.

Even if they are convicted of murder, they are usually out while they are still young enough to kill again. All too often they do just that.

Our prisons, thanks to years of liberalism, are often run by an evil compact between the stronger convicts and the unionised warders, which is why it is even easier to buy drugs in jail than at the gates of your local comprehensive school.

Witnesses are frightened into dropping their evidence and the law does not seem to have the power to protect them, or to punish those responsible.

Our weak and feeble system, in short, is a national disgrace. Wrong and evil flourish while the law-abiding are offered useless counselling and defeatist advice on fortifying their homes.

Instead of lecturing the Saudis, we might do well to demand real changes here, as soon as possible. Without hard reform, I predict that lawlessness will become so bad that the British people will sooner or later start voting for crowd-pleasing rabble-rousers who will offer us law and order in return for giving up our freedom.

If such people come to power they will make the Middle East's mullahs and ayatollahs look mild.

29/9/97

Let us call things by their proper names and stop using the horrible word "paedophile". Like many such expressions, it is designed to drain the true horror from what we are describing.

The Greek is just camouflage.

Millions of perfectly intelligent people can't even pronounce it. How many times have you heard a policeman or probation officer say "Peediofile" or even "Feedopile"?

So let us say "killers and child molesters" if that is what we are talking about. Then we shall be rightly enraged and baffled by a legal system which refuses to hang people who rape, torture and murder a little boy. And we will feel a decent wrath at a culture which treats their ugly actions as an illness. But then we treat all crime as an illness these days.

Once, within living memory, we were free people who knew that if we broke the law, we would be punished and disgraced. A man convicted of a crime would be sentenced immediately. He would then serve the sentence handed out with some time off if he behaved well inside.

And he would do so in an austere and disciplined place where order ruled.

Now, even the most blood-stained transgressors are remanded for weeks for "medical and social reports" as we seek to explain or even justify their misdeeds.

Then they are given a sentence which is a deliberate and calculated fraud, designed to deceive the public. They often serve as little as half of it.

As for "life" sentences, which the Lord Chief Justice so dislikes, they would be better described as "lie" sentences.

Thanks to years of weakness, the prison where they are sent is usually under the control of criminal gangs and drug salesmen. Thus innocent or nonviolent prisoners are condemned to an evil hell, while the foulest convicts know that they will be among friends, only mildly inconvenienced.

This is where years of fanciful, self-indulgent liberalism have got us.

Would we have so many "paedophiles" if we stopped calling them by pseudo-scientific names and if we revived those forgotten ideas – shame and punishment?

16/3/98

7

If you won't guard us, let us defend our homes

Why don't we have the right to defend our homes, since the police and the courts can't or won't do it for us? I never want to see another prosecution of a householder who has been driven half crazy by repeated attacks on his property and, as the hackneyed phrase goes, "taken the law into his own hands".

I am livid at the way the Crown Prosecution Service always seems to be keen to put such people in the dock, ruining their lives and reputations, while it is always finding excuses to let off career criminals.

It is no use the authorities complaining about "vigilantes" or snivelling about how it is the job of the police to deal with wrongdoers. That contract has been broken – by our liberal rulers.

Look at Green Gate Close in the Yorkshire town of Bolton upon Dearne. Only two of its 30 houses have not been robbed. Inside those houses, mostly occupied by old people, there is real fear. Windows are barred or nailed shut, even in the summer heat.

One old lady, gravely ill with cancer, no longer dares to leave her home, which has been violated four times by thieves. Another is often afraid to go to bed and is sometimes physically sick with fright as she listens for the all-too-familiar sound of some foul creature breaking in.

The local police say that this hellish place is not a crime black spot, which makes you wonder what happens in the really rough parts of Yorkshire.

But they are probably right. Mainly thanks to the pathetic failure of authority to combat drug use, there are now thousands of young men who use burglary to pay for their dope. If these thieves are caught, they are not punished. Mostly, they are not even caught.

In large parts of Britain nowadays, there is no effective law against burglary. It is accepted, like the climate, by those in power.

If the Tories wish to win the next election, I have an idea for them. The Home Secretary, and the Scottish authorities, should have the power to declare that, in certain zones, the police, the CPS and the courts are not efficient.

Until the police have resumed the round-the-clock, thorough foot patrols that are their main job, until the CPS starts prosecuting thieves and drug abusers and until the courts start punishing them in an effective fashion, it should be open season on burglars and vandals in these areas.

If a householder can prove that an attempt has been made to enter or damage his property, he or she will then be entitled to use reasonable force against the intruder or vandal and to seek assistance from his neighbours in using that force. No prosecution or lawsuit, public or private, should be allowed against such a householder.

Reasonable force should be generously redefined. There should be no pettifogging nonsense about whether the thief was trying to get in or out. If the thief is armed in any way, still greater force will be justified. Lawless, you say? taking the law into our own hands? vigilantism? Well, perhaps you are right. But when our own Government lets the law slip from its own hands, somebody else has to pick it up.

And what else can we do to help the people of Green Gate Close and all the other streets, avenues and crescents where peace and security are no more than a memory?

25/5/98

Legal hanging is far more civilised than this descent into barbarism

Just before Britain experienced its first lynch-mob killing in recent history in Manchester on Friday, our arrogant MPs abolished the death penalty for ever, by signing us up to the full provisions of the European Human Rights Convention.

Hanging can no longer even be debated by Parliament thanks to this sneaky little deed on Wednesday night.

How did your MP vote? I should ask if I were you.

Our half-wit liberal establishment will of course fail to see the connection between Parliament's action and the howling bloody mob, including women, who killed Stephen Mills with clubs, boots, fists and knives ignoring his pleas for mercy and pity.

Insulated from real life, the liberals have never come home to find a crack-smoker ransacking their bedrooms or a teenage truant kicking down their front doors. They do not keep a hammer or other weapon handy by their beds each night as millions of fearful householders now do.

They do not understand that the weakness of the penal system is a breach of the Government's contract with the people.

We, as ordinary citizens, must give up the fight to take revenge or act violently.

In return, our rulers are supposed to promise that they will do the revenging and provide a police force to prevent and deter crime. Yet, instead they have turned the police into a car- and helicopter-borne crime-reporting agency largely uninterested in patrolling the streets.

And they have made the prisons into revolving-door warehouses where those criminals dim enough to get caught are released after serving half their sentences.

Murder charges are bargained down to manslaughter for a quick cheap trial so that the man who butchers you tomorrow can be free to kill again still in the flower of his youth before you are 10 years dead.

Since the abolition of the death penalty armed crime figures have gone off the Home Office's charts. The homicide rate has climbed steadily and would have gone through the clouds if the modern NHS were not so good at dragging victims back from the doors of death.

I am disgusted by lynch law and condemn it. But I have

been predicting it for years and fear there will be more to come.

Lawful execution after due process is far more civilised than the gruesome descent into barbarism which is now well under way. It is unforgivable that MPs should have closed this option for ever especially in the name of "Human Rights". Is there no right to be free from fear?

25/5/98

Was this the week democracy began to die in this country? It may well have been. With a few honourable exceptions, MPs and Lords failed to stand up for their own rights or for ours. The shameful anti-terror law, which defines a terrorist as a murderer who has not yet had tea at Downing Street, was needless, crude, dangerous and squalid. Tony Benn was quite right to accuse the government of using the Commons as if it were the Supreme Soviet of some miserable people's democracy.

Look what it is doing and plans to do: break up the UK, bully Parliament with unfairly conducted referenda, turn the Queen into a Downing Street puppet, abolish the independent element of the Lords, change the rules of evidence to allow hearsay into court, confiscate the property of convicted people, introduce identity cards disguised as driving licences, give political parties virtual veto over MP selection, turn the Cabinet into a rubber stamp, put political commissars into every ministry, hand over economic powers and tax rates to a foreign politburo.

If anyone did all these things in one night people would say there had been a coup d'etat. Is it any better because it's happening in slow motion?

7/9/98

What is wrong with our police? Let me stress here that I believe most policemen are good and decent men trying to do a job made impossible by stupid laws and by blockhead graduate leaders who think they are social workers in helmets.

It is not the ordinary copper's fault that our police service has taken over from British Rail as our most lamentable nationalised industry. Home Office "experts" who, back in 1967, decided to take constables off the beat have much to answer for. So does Lady Thatcher, who poured cash into the police service without asking for much in return, and who allowed the force to be hamstrung by bureaucracy and evidence rules designed by police-baiting liberals.

Whatever the reason, there is no justification for the disappearance of foot patrols from streets and parks (where their presence might have saved some trouble for the Government this week).*

You will often hear chief constables moaning about their stretched resources. Pay no attention. This column commissioned its own research and discovered this:

In 1968, when they still walked the beat there were 91,538 police officers in England and Wales, backed up by 19,818 civilian staff. This year there are 126,944 police officers, backed up by 53,480 civilian staff.

So where have they all gone? Why are they never visible except in the Houses of Parliament or at football matches and bypass protests? Seminars, special squads, computer training, suing each other at sex discrimination tribunals or seeking compensation and early retirement, that's my guess.

2/11/98

Beggars

I am unfair, unjust and prejudiced about beggars. Sometimes I give them money but it is to make me feel better about myself,

---

* The resignation of the Welsh Secretary after he was robbed in unclear circumstances on Clapham Comon.

rather than because I believe I am doing any good.

Sometimes I hurry harshly by, I am sure I often give to undeserving thieves and just as sure that I occasionally spurn true hardship.

I get angry with them especially if they have tiny children on display, suspecting them of cynical fraud.

If they *are* phoneys they are, of course, committing a terrible sin poisoning the wells of charity in a world that is already callous enough.

I am haunted by the terrible warning issued by Jesus himself, advising us against callousness with the words "Insomuch as ye have done it unto the least of one of these, ye have done it unto Me".

And at this time of year I am also frightened by the lament of Marley's ghost, dragging a great chain forged by his own stinginess in life.

I suspect that the truly needy, the respectable elderly huddled in unheated loneliness, would die rather than beg, yet they need my money and my sympathy far more than the gaunt but healthy figures who hang around bridges and stairways with their miserable dogs and mangy blankets.

As our big city police have pretty much given up enforcing laws against them, there are now so many of these wretched sights that this has become an everyday problem for most of us.

This week, at a big London underground station, I was wrestling ineptly with a ticket machine when a young man appeared at my elbow asking for change. Applying my usual crude and prejudiced standards. I summed him up. Filthy matted hair and clothes not just scruffy but carefully calculated to repel any normal employer. Not a chance.

"Sorry, no," I told him politely and quietly. The next thing I knew, he was taunting me with a fusillade of short foul words and jabbing his finger at me. For a moment he turned away to pester a young woman at a cash-point machine. Probably foolishly, but to take the pressure off her I called out to him to leave her alone.

By now I was standing in a ticket queue (having lost my battle with the machine), a heavy suitcase in each hand. He swerved back and began jeering obscenely and jabbing again so close to my face that I could feel the air tremble against my cheek. I told him to go away or I would call the police.

My fellow members of the public acted as if nothing was happening, something I have come to rely on if there is danger or embarrassment in the offing. A few feet away, three strapping railway officials in luminous jackets and peaked caps looked on uselessly.

As he pursued me to the barrier still bawling verbal slime and poking his fingers close to my eye, I urged these imposing persons to do or even say something. They muttered feebly about not having the right training. When I suggested that this was a poor excuse, they turned on me. One called me an arrogant bastard, which may well be true but did not seem to me to be the point.

I grew up believing that this great and kind country would never allow any of its citizens to starve or freeze. I still believe that this should be so, and is so. If I am right then authority is entitled to arrest these people, discover their true circumstances and either see that they are housed and fed, or punish them for cruel trickery.

The current attitude of blind-eye tolerance, combined with a half-hearted impersonal charity which is a sour mix of guilt and fear, is dishonest, dishonourable and worthy of a Third World slum state.

16/12/96

THE EURO ROUBLE

The trouble with Germany is that – like Chancellor Helmut Kohl himself – it is much too big for its own good. If it were a little country such as Holland or Denmark, we would all admire its superb beer, charming half-timbered towns, quaint myths and lovely music.

We would be close to raptures about its recent discovery of democracy and the rule of law, its new-found tolerance, its effective state schools, its cultured, intelligent and sympathetic elite classes.

Even in recession, it is an enviable place. Any Briton visiting the Federal Republic will quickly find that a German slump is much more comfortable than a British boom. Nasty people survive there, as the recent fire-bomb attack on a foreigners' hostel in Lubeck showed, and there is not much comfort for the Turkish guest-workers who will never be allowed to become fully German. But fears of some sort of Nazi resurgence are overblown.

No, the problem for Helmut's united state is that its huge shadow spreads across time and space, in dark memories and dark fears of an unknown future. Even in the best of hands, this mighty nation is bound to be an awkward neighbour.

Because it sprawls plumply from France to Poland, and from the Baltic to the Swiss Alps; because it is so rich in heavy, imposing ways – order, precision, discipline, punctuality; and above all because it has proved twice that it can hold Europe in the palm of its mailed fist, Germany cannot yet be quite like other nations.

That is why it was so wrong and so foolish for Herr Kohl to try to make our flesh creep with his "War and Peace" oration in Belgium, a speech so ill-judged that it may come to mark the high tide of his influence over Europe.

We all know without being reminded that Germany has sought again and again to dominate the continent through bullying use of her power.

But we thought all that was over. We thought that a new Germany, free and prosperous, had learned to control herself.

But in this oddly menacing speech, Chancellor Kohl seemed to be warning that, if the old Germany breaks loose again, it will be our fault for not doing as we were told. This line has a queasy, familiar ring to it.

He was even clumsy enough to mention his country's two invasions of Belgium – in 1914 and 1940 – as if his hosts did not know all about them. They know. The Dutch know. The French know. The Danes and the Czechs and the Poles know. All have living memories of the treacherous and violent years when rivers of grey steel burst through their lawful borders in pursuit of the ultimate Teutonic dream.

And they know what that dream turned out to be – medieval plunder, perverted science, the fabled German idealism of Goethe and Schiller and Hegel, only harnessed to an evil ideal.

Now, in the most amazing piece of nerve, he stands up and tells us that it is only German wisdom that keeps us from yet another European war. Listen to the vanity of it: "European integration is in reality a question of war and peace in the 21st Century. We have no desire to return to the nation state of old. It cannot solve the great problems of the 21st Century. Nationalism has brought too great suffering to our continent."

Well, up to a point. German nationalism has certainly done so, but Britain's nationalism, her determination to defend her sovereignty and that of other democratic nations, has twice saved Europe from becoming a Greater German Reich.

Worse, in a piece of rhino-skinned tactlessness, he compares Britain to the slowest ship in a convoy. What he wanted to say was that we would not be allowed to delay progress towards his Euro-dream.

What he actually succeeded in doing was to remind

millions about Germany's two ruthless attempts to starve this country into submission through unrestricted submarine warfare. And what a strange metaphor it is anyway. A convoy that does not stay together is doomed to destruction, as a few grizzled old U-boat commanders could tell him over a glass or two of rough corn schnapps.

But this is only part of a greater arrogance on Chancellor Kohl's part. Dizzy after successfully swallowing East Germany, does he now yearn to be a new Charlemagne, dispensing peace and culture to an admiring continent?

If so, he will have to learn some history. Like many other Eurocrats, he makes claims for the European Union which simply have no base in fact. Western Europe has been at peace since 1945 not because of Brussels, but because of Washington.

It was NATO, not the European Union, which successfully suppressed our continent's ancient rivalries after Britain grew too weak to do so. It was NATO which kept the Russians out, the Germans down and the Americans in. It was NATO which allowed the French to joke: "We like Germany so much that we are delighted there are now two of them."

It was united Europe, left to its own devices, which helped plunge Yugoslavia into war by bowing to German pressure to give unwarranted and impracticable recognition to unstable rival statelets. It was NATO, or what is now left of it, which then imposed peace. He might also learn some other lessons from across the Atlantic. The United States, the world's most successful federal state, has been anything but peaceful. Riven by mistrust for years after independence, America did not become a single nation until after one of the bloodiest and most destructive civil wars in history.

This was a speech too far. No democratic leader should allow himself to utter threats of war against his neighbours, even in such vague, prophetic terms. It will only fuel the fears of those who believe that the new Germany wishes to dominate Europe through the deutschmark, only because it is easier and cheaper than crushing the continent with the Wehrmacht.

Do we now have to accept this use of power is an inevitable force of nature? Is it the fate of 21st-century Europe either to accept orders from reunited Berlin, or to hope for rescue from across the Atlantic, which may not come again? Surely we – and the people of Germany – can do better than this. There are higher purposes in Europe than mere economic union. One is to strengthen democracy, which has always been the best guarantee against war.

Another is to find ways in which differing and powerful cultures, such as Britain and Germany, can learn from each other and share the benefits instead of wasting their energy on fruitless rivalry and conflict.

5/2/96

The Patriot Game

Try to defend British national interests in front of anyone who thinks he is an intellectual, such as most BBC interviewers or the Tory MP George Walden, and you can guarantee that the words "xenophobia", "Little England" and "flag-waving" will be flung at you within seconds. "I cannot really be associated with a petty-minded nationalist party," snaps Mr Walden, as he complains of something called "cheap patriotism".

He sounds as if he is afraid that people will think he is wearing Union Jack underpants. Perhaps Mr Walden prefers expensive, discreet, hand-tailored patriotism of a special kind that can only be bought and used by gentlemen with good university degrees. On the other hand, perhaps he finds the whole idea of loving his own country rather embarrassing and best left to others. For him, for the BBC and for anyone else who may want to know, we present an easy cut-out-and-keep guide to the difference between defending your national interest and xenophobia.

Xenophobia

Literally a fear of strangers, especially common in Continental Europe, and recently on display in the Balkans, where harmless people in their thousands were raped, murdered, burnt out of their homes, imprisoned and forced into exile because they had a different religion from their neighbours or used a different alphabet.

Sometimes this sort of hatred is also motivated by lust for territory. Often, it takes place in parts of the world where the people have no sense of belonging to a proper nation, only to a tribe. Other major instances since 1900 include: Russian pogroms against Jews with the tacit support of the Tsarist authorities; Stalin's mass deportations of Tatars, Chechens and Baltic peoples; Turkish slaughter of Armenians; Azerbaijani pogroms against Armenians in Baku; German mass-murder of Jews, Poles, gypsies and Russians; bloody ethnic cleansing of Germans after World War Two from Czech and Polish territory; persecution of the Hungarian minority in Romania.

In Belgium, heart of the "internationalist" European Union, there are bitter divisions between Flemings and Walloons, which have fortunately stopped short of major violence. Outside Northern Ireland, where the conflict is almost incomprehensible to most Britons, xenophobia has been almost unknown in the British Isles in recent centuries.

Patriotism

A reasonable but emotional attachment to one's own country, especially strong in Europe's two oldest nations, Britain and France. In peacetime expressed as a love of landscape, literature, shared history, traditions, strengthened by the memory of past triumphs. In wartime often expressed with irony or nostalgia ("There'll always be an England, while there's a country lane..."), rather than loud passion.

In Britain it traditionally unites all classes, ever since the battles of Agincourt, Poitiers and Crecy, where English peasant archers fought with Norman noblemen against a common foe, and the aristocrats, for the first time, found that they needed their fellow countrymen. In Britain, patriotism is largely unspoken because an island nation does not normally need to distinguish itself from neighbours by noisy display.

It can be one of the most powerful, unselfish emotions, sometimes terribly misused but often a great force for good. It was crucial to British survival in 1940, to the recovery of Russia from near-defeat by the Nazis in 1941 and vital for the eventual rescue of democracy in Europe. Combined with devout Roman Catholicism, Polish patriotism also helped to overthrow the Soviet Empire. In Czechoslovakia, also, love of country played a great part in the "Velvet Revolution" against communism in 1989.

28/5/96

Pride in a national vision

The trouble with many of our Brussels-loving classes is that they do not really like Britain or the British very much. Look at Sir Edward Heath or Lord Jenkins as they explain their pro-Market machinations in Michael Elliott's marvellous BBC2 series *The Poisoned Chalice*.

They both seem to be passionless men who would be embarrassed to find themselves, say, in a crowd of lower-middle-class royalists as the Queen Mother goes by, or next to a softly weeping war veteran on Remembrance Sunday.

Yet in truth they are fervent revolutionaries, determined to "modernise" this country with waves of cultural revolution until it is unrecognisable. Jenkins changed our moral climate forever with his permissive society. Heath's costly and grandiose local government reforms swept away much that was old and loved, and replaced it with ugly, artificial things which were supposed to be better but weren't.

In post-war Europe both men saw that the bland,

bureaucratic steam-roller of the Brussels Commission was the dedicated enemy of the ramshackle, disorganised, conservative but uniquely free Britain that they seem to have despised. In other times and places, men like these might actually have joined revolutionary movements because of their dislike of tradition and their desire for radical change. Revolutionaries, of course, loathe patriotism because it is a far more powerful force than their own. They are very fond of international movements and world bodies such as the United Nations, which seek to undermine national, conservative feeling.

Like all world reformers, such people are certain that they are right, and tend to believe that their opponents must have something wrong with them personally.

Hence the abuse which they like to heap on patriots. But what does it really mean? They sneer at "flag-waving", but what is so bad about occasionally waving your flag, especially if it is an international symbol of justice and freedom?

Americans of Left and Right happily fly their flag above their front doors, sing their national anthem at sporting events. They would be baffled if anyone criticised them for it.

The Euro-fanatics talk about "Little Englanders" but do not realise that this was originally a term of abuse aimed at people like themselves. The original "Little Englanders" opposed the growth of the British Empire, preferring this country to turn its back on the world beyond the Continent.

But the truth is that Britain has always prospered most when she has had little to do with her immediate neighbours. Our great expansions of wealth and power came in the years when Spain or France kept us out by force. If we had been the insular, foreigner-hating people we are accused of being, would we then have set out across the globe to trade and colonise?

The opposite is true. The USA, Canada, Australia and New Zealand are tributes to our adventurous and outward-looking nature. The democracy and free institutions of independent India are evidence that we were not crude conquerors and exploiters, but bringers of light and freedom.

There is hardly a language or a culture in the world which has not had some influence on us, hardly a spot on the globe where British explorers or traders have not stood.

And yet, because we do not wish to trust our destinies to platoons of paper shufflers in a mist-girt concrete city in some patriotism-free zone in the Low Countries, they dare to call us xenophobes and tell us that our honest emotions are cheap.
28/5/96

Proud to be British . . . proud to be European

Let me get something straight with one of the other squatters on this noble column, who wrote here last week as if those who disliked the European Union hated Europe.

I have held in my hand my great grandfather's certificate of naturalisation as a British subject. He was a German Jew, who wisely decided to leave his native Prussia 70 years before the final solution.

About the same time another great grandfather left his ancestral village in Wiltshire for the industrial clamour of Portsmouth. Stalin would have called me a rootless cosmopolitan. Hitler would have called me "Mixed Race, 2nd grade", and both would have done Continental things to me had I been in their power. Despite this, and perhaps because of my genes, I feel at home in the historic lands of old Prussia, Russia and Austria.

My heart also lifts when I step off the boat in France, and I am seldom happier than when I am half-lost in the deepest and most French parts of that country.

I know the difference between the EU (15 countries) and Europe (47 nations), because I have travelled all across the mighty continent, from Ireland's Atlantic Coast to the Ural Mountains, and from Iceland to the Caucasus.

My father voyaged even further and this Boxing Day I shall be remembering with pride that he was at the sinking of the German battlecruiser *Scharnhorst* off the North Cape on December 26, 1943, helping to save Europe from tyranny. I am profoundly European, because I am profoundly British. I am sorry so many of our Continental neighbours cannot feel the same pride and wish they could, but see no reason to give up my own.

24/12/96

Everything you ever need to know about the Euro

The Chancellor says we should get ready for it. Big business likes it, small business doesn't. Both the main political parties are split on it. Yet nobody ever seems to say what it is, so here are the vital questions you've always wanted to ask and the answers you need...

Q. What is it?
A. A plan to merge the money and the economies of the major West European nations.

Q. When?
A. Very soon now. Those taking part will lock their currencies together on January 1, 1999. New notes and coins will be issued on January 1, 2002. The countries involved will abolish their own money on July 1, 2002.

Q. How much will it be worth and what will it be called?
A. Worth around 75 pence★ the Euro will be divided into 100 cents.

_____

★This really was true at the time

Q. Can you get out of it once you are in?
A. No, never.

Q. Who will run it?
A. The European Central Bank, based in Frankfurt.

Q. What about the politicians?
A. The rules say that the bank should be completely independent of politics. But the French and Germans – whose idea the whole thing is – keep rowing about this.

Q. Will Britain take part?
A. Impossible to say. This depends on a referendum.

Q. Will we suffer by staying out?
A. Yes. If the new currency does well and is a success, we will be even more on the margins of the European Union than we are already and may be forced to join on bad terms late in the day. If the new currency is a flop or wobbles, the pound will rise as investors get out of the Euro and into Sterling. This will hit our exports.

Q. Will we suffer by going in?
A. Yes, very likely. But probably not immediately. If the doubters are right (read on) most of the bad effects will take time to work through. By that time, though, it will be too late to get out.

Q. What are its benefits?
A. For those trading or travelling inside the EU, there could be big savings. No more moneychangers, no more export contracts turning nasty because the pound has risen or fallen too much.

Q. Is that all?
A. That all depends what you mean by a benefit. European leaders – such as German Chancellor Helmut Kohl – say openly that a united currency will lead to a United Europe

much like the USA, producing peace, stability and plenty and abolishing the danger of war in the world's most unstable continent. Its British supporters tend to dwell on the economic benefits, perhaps because they think that British voters do not much fancy the idea of a United States of Europe.

Q. Sounds harmless. Why should anyone be against it?
A. Like the Pros, the Antis have two arguments – practical, and political.

Q. The practical problems?
A. Small businesses without much export business get nothing out of it but they still have to pay the costs of switching. British shops alone face conversion costs of £3.5 billion.

Q. Isn't that worth it, to avoid all those fluctuations?
A. Only if you trade exclusively with European Union countries. The Euro rate against the dollar and the yen will still go up and down. The British Government and the Bank of England will have no power to influence it. Britain's mid-Atlantic economy has much more trade with the USA than the rest of Europe, so the European Central Bank won't take much notice of our needs.

Q. But surely we will be part of a strong and prosperous Europe if we join. Germany is a success story. Won't we benefit from its wealth?
A. Possibly the other way round. Germany is in a mess at the moment because its labour costs are high and its economy is out of step with ours. Many European countries have very shaky economies but are still being allowed to join. Perhaps most important of all, the French, German and Italian states have promised their workers pensions worth billions of pounds but have set aside no money to pay them.

If we merge our economy with them now, our North Sea oil and gas reserves could end up paying the pensions of millions of Germans, French and Italians. And our savings, converted to Euros, would be affected by their inflation.

Q. Oh, come on, the Americans have one currency for the whole USA and they have the world's most successful economy. Surely this is just moaning?
A. True, up to a point, but Americans have a single language and legal system. If you lose your job in New York, you can move to California. But if you're on the dole in Manchester, you can't easily move to Munich, let alone find work there. Experts fear the Euro could create permanent pools of unemployment, where people are trapped.

Q. And the political objections?
A. The doubters say that monetary union is the first step in a political union, the creation of a superstate in which Britain will lose her independence. They warn that the European Central Bank will be so powerful that Europe-wide political institutions will have to be created to balance it.

Q. I still can't make my mind up. What should I do?
A. This is a grave and important matter, far more so than decimalisation. It will affect you and your children personally and deeply. Start taking an interest now so that nobody can pull the wool over your eyes when Referendum Day finally arrives.

Know what you are voting for... or against. It is your duty as a citizen and it will be no excuse, if you don't like the outcome, to say you couldn't be bothered.
11/11/97

We don't have to walk into Blair's Euro trap

The National Suicide Plan announced by Princess Tony is a warning that the present Government *must* be removed from office at the next election. By deliberately prejudging the result of the vote on abolishing the pound, the plan serves notice that this promised referendum will be worthless.

If we dare to say No, then the referendum will simply be held again and again until we come up with what Princess Tony thinks is the right answer.

If, on the other hand, we are browbeaten into saying Yes, that will be the end of the matter for ever, as the trap smashes down on our spine, 1,000 years of independence come to an end and we begin our new existence as a subject province of Euroland.

I cannot say often enough that the next election is the decisive moment in our national history. If Princess Tony wins it, it will be the end of Britain, for ever and ever. So who cares if you don't like William Hague's bald pate, or his accent, or didn't enjoy the last Tory government? Voting is not an act of conscience and principle, it is a practical choice between bad and atrocious.

I don't know whether the Princess himself actually understands what he plans to do to this country. But what about the bright ones in the back room? Can they really believe the piffle and tripe which issues from their pens?

It is frightening to read the pitiful, ignorant and trivial arguments put forward by the supporters of the Euro-Rouble. Can they truly be convinced by this thin stuff or are they just hiding their real views?

Whenever I debate it, I am astonished by the lack of either passion or understanding among the supporters of the new Rouble. I am often left thinking that I, who loathe it, could make a better case for the Euro than they do.

If you really can't work out that cars are cheaper on the continent because they're priced in another currency then I pity you when you try to buy a beer abroad. If you really think that big economies are any safer from slumps than small ones, then it's back to kindergarten economics class for you.

And, if you really think that having a single currency makes a nation out of rivals, then kindly explain a) the American Civil War, b) Yugoslavia and c) the often violent break-up of the USSR.

As for "it's inevitable", it's only inevitable if we vote for it, and we don't have to. Why should we, the fifth largest economy in the world, have to snuff out our independence just because someone else has started a new and rather dodgy currency?

But the one that takes the prize is the suggestion that joining this thing will give us more "influence" in Brussels. Influence over what? There is no argument in the EU, except over just how much corruption it will tolerate, how big the damaging subsidies will be, how much higher the unemployment and the taxes will rise.

They resent and despise our free economy and low taxes. But they would quite like to steal all the business which now goes through the City of London.

And they want our oil, our gold and our big fat pension funds to help shore up their crumbling pyramid of waste and folly.

1/3/99

A rescue party has finally dug me out from the snowdrift of adjectives which engulfed me on Wednesday when my colleague Andrew Marr gave me a piece of his mind. My views on Europe are, he says, "violently hostile, rancid, nostalgic, self-pitying, pessimistic, defeatist, nervous, retreating and anti-European".

I must reply, since Andrew is a man I respect and whose words cannot be ignored. This is my response to him.

Why are you so keen on abolishing the pound? It is common ground between us that this choice is a decisive moment in our history. It is also common ground between our two sides that it will damage our economy.

Your faction stated in its pro-Brussels campaign in 1975, that "there was a threat to employment in Britain from the movement in the Common Market towards an Economic and

Monetary Union. This could have forced us to accept fixed exchange rates for the pound, restricting industrial growth and so putting jobs at risk. This threat has been removed."

The laws of economics do not change. If it was a threat to jobs in 1975, it is one now. Is throwing your fellow citizens onto the dole a price worth paying for your ideals?

What exactly are those ideals? On the Continent, the supporters of the single currency say boldly that they intend to create a new superstate. The real power in the Social Democrat-dominated German Government, Oskar Lafontaine, says: "The United States of Europe has been the aim of the Social Democratic Party all along."

Yet nowhere in more than a thousand words do you openly state that you desire this. Why not? Do you think that the British people would not like it?

Your case hangs on some highly optimistic claims. You say the EU will somehow "evolve" into a "confederation of states with strong national governments and a more political, less bureaucratic, central regime". How will this happen? Which powerful factions in the EU are in favour of it?

You think this is likelier than the "Germanic superstate" which you rightly say that I fear.

Well, I am not alone. Theo Waigel, finance minister in the last German Government, says "Germany, as the biggest and most powerful economic member state, will be the leader, whether we like it or not."

You say that Britain has prospered through contact and trade with the outside world. I agree. But that is quite different from handing control of our economy to outside powers.

You say we do not have total control over that economy. Of course we haven't. But it doesn't follow from this that we should give up any control over it. On the contrary, it means that we should guard what limited powers we do have with special care. Can you name a single significant independent country which doesn't have its own currency?

You say that, had Britain joined the European scheme earlier we might have won a better deal. Possibly. But possibly not.

In nearly 30 years we have failed to change the basic nature of the beast. We have not won back our stolen fishing grounds, we have not reformed the mad farm policy, we have not prised France and Germany free from their tight lovers' embrace. What evidence do you have that this will now change? Who will Britain's allies be?

The only progress we have made, in winning a rebate, has come from being as tough and selfish as the French. But when they do it, it's all right, and when we do it, everyone in Brussels says we're "anti-European".

As for that charge made against me, it's a funny sort of anti-European who takes his young family to live in Moscow and who has travelled with delight from the River Shannon to the Ural Mountains, from Reykjavik to Gibraltar.

I love the place. I just don't want to be ruled by it. Why do you?

8/3/99

CULTURE/MORALS

The stone, flung covertly and accurately, hit me hard on the side of the head.

It was the clearest possible answer to the questions I had been asking.

The missile came after I had spent time trying to find out what goes on in the minds of the young barbarians who have turned an ordinary housing estate into a place of fear, fire and hate.

Why, I asked them, did they steal cars, smash windows, trample gardens, drive old ladies from their homes?

How would they like it if others did the same to them? Would anything scare them into stopping?

They were boastful yet evasive, especially one pair of pitiful youths who hid their pinched faces with IRA-style balaclavas.

Yes, it was them, no, it wasn't – ha, ha, ha.

Until the stone struck, I had not fully understood how savage these yahoos really are.

We were gathered round a bonfire on the Manor Estate in Sheffield – once a homely, peaceful, unremarkable community.

Now it is a place where dusk brings fear into the lives of many.

Again and again, old people begged me to keep their identities secret as they recounted their miseries.

One told me: "My neighbour came, trembling, to my front door. She was not just scared stiff, she was scared to death. She left the next day."

The menace comes from a floating gang of youths who humiliate the old and the weak, women without husbands, anybody vulnerable.

It may seem trivial from a distance – they gather in noisy, menacing knots in the street, playing football in carefully-tended front gardens, responding to protests with streams of filthy words and threats.

But their victims have the lined, sleepless look of real fear about them.

Those who do not cringe and submit find their windows broken, their fences wrecked, heaps of excrement in their gardens.

If that fails, their garden sheds are demolished and burned, their children's bicycles stolen, their cars wrecked.

"Like all old people, I had longed for a bungalow," said one victim.

He pointed to his handsome, newly-built house, one of many recently put up on the estate.

It showed all the signs of love and care. He and his wife have lived in the area for the past 33 years, and would have liked to stay. Not now.

"My doctors have told me that if I get one more big angina attack then it's hospital.

"I can't risk that. I can't leave my wife on her own in a place like this, with people like this.

"Our hopes are all smashed down. We have to surrender to idiotic young kids."

Others, glancing round to see if they are watched, emerge from behind their doors to confirm the reign of terror.

Not that they need to. At the top end of the estate, it seems almost half the houses are now empty.

Some are boarded up, many have special steel sheeting, like something out of wartime, clamped across their front windows.

These days, the council or the housing association seal up empty dwellings within 30 minutes of the tenants leaving.

They have to, or the gangs take their final revenge.

One house is a ruin, its charred rafters stark against the sky. Another has a garden full of wrecked and shredded furniture.

When the fire brigade come, the gangs throw bricks at them. They want to see things burn unchecked.

"Welcome to Hell" says a scrawled, triumphant message on the boarded-up houses near the steel-shuttered shops and the dead street lamps. A greasy coil of black smoke rolls across the street from yet another fire.

In the middle of all this a brave man works. The local Anglican vicar the Rev Richard Atkinson tries to defend decency in what is fast becoming a moral desert.

His brand-new £750,000 church was supposed to be a declaration of faith in the area. Just the other night some young mind took a hammer to its windows.

You can feel the wanton hatred in the hand that wielded that hammer.

Stained glass depictions of good things – a mother and child, a country scene, a coal miner, a symbolic window embodying faith in the city itself – have all been wrecked.

Mr Atkinson, one of the few people who has tried to talk to the yobs, and to understand them, is grieved.

As an ice-cream van patrols the blighted streets tinkling Greensleeves, he explains why some houses are targeted and not others.

"They pick on those who stand up for themselves; those who stick out in some way."

His boss, Archdeacon Stephen Lowe, says "There is a complete breakdown of society here." But Mr Atkinson, a thoughtful priest, does not reach for the standard formulas.

"It isn't just about money," he said. "I actually do think it's about people having to change their hearts and minds.

"Until there is a change of heart in which you have some concern for others, and not just for yourself, there are limits to what you are going to achieve." I watched him trying to make sense of the young men and women who crowded noisily near his damaged church, swigging from bottles of strong lager.

They seem mystified by his kindness.

27/10/95

What if reading and writing became a minority activity, an accomplishment like playing a musical instrument, rather than an unavoidable part of modern life? What if a solid volume of print becomes as mysterious to our descendants as the carved front of Lincoln Cathedral, or the great windows of Chartres are to us?

As we look with despair at the new school test results, with their dismal evidence of semi-literate children, we tend to blame the usual suspects – bad teachers if you are John Major, too little school spending if you are Tony Blair, not enough grammar school places if you are Harriet Harman.

But the real explanation may be much more serious, a sign of a deep change in our way of life which has gone so far that it is too late to stop.

The children who scored badly on the tests are the same ones who cope brilliantly with the technology of the home. They can use the microwave, programme the video, run up giant scores on computer games.

They can navigate happily through an airport or a supermarket, helped by picture-signs which were designed to aid foreigners but are just as useful to the non-reader. The new Euro-world, in which we are not expected to be able to speak or read the local language, has had the side-effect of making it easier to be an illiterate.

They are already familiar with the telephone, once a rather forbidding and expensive machine. Unlike their parents, they will be undaunted by faxes, answering machines and voice-mail systems.

It is a fascinating feature of modern life that the young and unread find it far easier to cope with the strange logic of computers and microchips than those who grew up in the age of print.

Uncluttered by fixed ideas about how things should work or how they used to work, they accept them on their own terms.

They are not wrapped in some sort of total darkness. They can all read enough to get by, to decipher road signs or newspaper headlines, or work out the name of the cereal they are eating. They could probably read a lot more and a lot better if they wanted to.

But we have made a world in which they can live a perfectly adequate life without having to read fluently or for any length of time – except at school.

Just as the calculator has destroyed the will of millions to learn arithmetic, the new multimedia have taken away the incentive to take up reading as a significant occupation.

So for many of the next generation, the classroom is the only place where they are expected to take these cumbersome hieroglyphics seriously. There are no books to speak of at home, and if there were they would not read them.

Crucially, they no longer see books as the source of all knowledge. They used to have an honoured place in many homes where they have long ago been shouldered aside by various multimedia devices, from the TV set to the CD-ROM.

And this is not just a problem for the new semi-literates at the bottom of the education system. The printed word is losing its power over much of the middle class as well.

Once films were made out of books. Now it is the other way round. In America last year, the new film version of Louisa May Alcott's *Little Women* was a surprise success. But if young people wanted to go on to read the story, they were able to do so in a novelised version of the film. It was not necessary to go back to the original text.

This was also the year of the first multimedia memoirs. One of Richard Nixon's aides published his damaging account of the White House years both as a book and as a CD-ROM.

The CD-ROM buyers felt they had got the better bargain, for their package contained whole clips of old home-movies from the time, cunningly inserted in the text.

It was no longer necessary for the reader to imagine the events of the past. He could see and hear them taking place, sometimes accompanied by mood-inducing music.

Even the supposed great classics of the language, Shakespeare and the King James Bible, are read less and less in the original. The Bible is modernised and paraphrased. Shakespeare's plays are turned into clever comic strips or transformed (however brilliantly) into movies.

Better this than that they should die altogether, but most people never read them at all, and many only see and hear these works through someone else's eyes, at second hand.

This is a world which seems to have great promise. It is convenient, efficient – as long as the computers do not fail – brightly-coloured and limitless. But it is also strangely shallow and flat. That most powerful human faculty, imagination, is discarded and replaced with soothing noise and sweet colour, made in a laboratory or a studio.

Whether we want this or not, it looks as if we are going to get it. The book trade, for all its prizes and huge advance payments to star authors, is battling to survive as it turns itself into a branch of show business. Visit a bookshop these days and you will find that the actual selection on offer grows narrower month by month.

Public libraries, anxious to keep some sort of role, have given over much of their shelving to video rentals. But we have not yet reached the point imagined in Ray Bradbury's book *Fahrenheit 451*, in which it is a crime to own books, and the job of firemen to burn them on sight.

Perhaps closer is Nigel Kneale's grim Eighties TV fantasy of the near future, *Quatermass*, in which books are sold as fuel for cooking and heating in a country which has run out of oil. It never even occurs to anybody to *read* them.

The less we want to read, the less we shall be able to do so. A whole world of beauty, adventure, mystery and morality will be closed to all but an elite few. The prayer we should be offering up today is for the rebirth of the written word.

26/1/96

The sad death of Caroline Bacon, the 14-year-old girl given the contraceptive pill without her parents' knowledge and consent, is the latest incident in the fierce war now raging between the family and its most bitter enemy, the State.

Leave aside for the moment the unhappy question of what sort of civilisation hands out hormones to innocents. Pass over the fact that a 14-year-old was being aided and abetted in taking part in an illegal act, for sexual intercourse under the age of 16 is still an offence under criminal law.

Because for Caroline's angry and stricken parents, there is a much more painful question. Who took away their sacred right and duty to protect their little girl from harm?

Those who have, or even hope to have, the joy of raising children know that this is the greatest responsibility and heaviest charge of their lives. From the moment of birth, parents are never free of anxiety for their young. In return, they have – or ought to have – equally unique powers to teach, warn and guard.

This is as it should be. But in recent years, the cold shadow of authority has fallen between parent and child in ways never before dreamed of in a free society. The impact of this change has been increased by the divorce epidemic, by the growth of a money-spinning "youth culture" of music, entertainment, food and clothing, and by the hugely-expanded powers of social workers under the Children Act.

Every parent has felt it. Children who should still be cushioned from the world by ideas of imagination, adventure and romance come home from school with their heads stuffed with information about the mechanics of sex.

Attempts to rein in children can be, and often are, thwarted by the hugely-exaggerated cult of "Child Abuse", so that any child is free to denounce its parents – and be believed – in a way not seen since the death of Stalin.

And, of course, the missionaries of the Family Planning lobby are always waiting in their smiley shame-free clinics with their happy advice leaflets and their cupboards bulging with free anti-baby devices. Their implicit message is, as it has always been, the outdated, untrue and selfish notion that sex is just a recreation, like tennis.

Even the wildest and most savage pre-Christian societies at least linked sexual abandon with fertility. Our 20th-century paganism is the first to link it with sterility.

And perhaps it is because we take the matter so lightly that we take too little notice of the risks. If we realised the enormity of what the Pill does to a woman's body, we might be considerably more careful about using it.

Caroline Bacon's parents, by definition, would have taken more care of her than the nameless medic who gave her the Pill (contraceptives are invariably given away for nothing at an annual cost of £50 million for the Pill alone, an interesting reflection on our national priorities).

Her mother Jennifer says: "If she'd come to me we could have talked it over and I'd have been able to warn her of the possible dangers. *But no one gave me the chance*."

Of course, the reason why she was not given the chance is that the new morality fears what parents might say. It fears that they may offer guidance on right and wrong, good and evil. These are concepts which it wants to banish from the neat, shiny, concrete, glass and steel world which it still hopes to create.

And here a fascinating point arises. You may be under the impression that a doctor must always maintain a priest-like silence when he prescribes the Pill to some under-age tot. This is not so. He may not tell the parents, but he may tell the authorities if he suspects "abuse".

In a pamphlet issued by the BMA and several other respectable organisations, the following advice is given to doctors: "No patient, adult or minor, has an absolute right to complete confidentiality in all circumstances. Confidentiality must be balanced against society's interest in protecting vulnerable people from serious harm."

It goes on to say: "In exceptional circumstances, the doctor may believe that the young person seeking medical advice on sexual matters is being exploited or abused."

Nothing wrong with that, but why is sexual abuse a good

38

enough excuse, while the concern of parents is not? Mainly because the fear of "abuse" and "society's interest" now carries more weight than the rights of the family to govern itself.

The permissive lobby does offer one powerful argument for their interference. They point to hard cases like the 12-year-old girl who recently became pregnant, and say that surely such a child would have been better off if she had been on the Pill.

Hard cases do make bad law. If a 12-year-old's childhood has been so utterly debauched, there is no guarantee that she would use any devices given to her. Perhaps more important, if our society did not smile so generously on the feckless young and their illegal sex, if we could reintroduce children to ideas such as shame and responsibility and parental power, it would surely be a better protection than the new order of the Pill and condom and sex education?

Anyway, is this new order working on its own terms? We only need to ask the question to know the answer. In a society where few people over the age of nine do not know in detail how babies are made, we have 160,000 abortions a year and 137,000 under-age girls gulping contraceptives with their cornflakes. In England alone, clinics issue around 80,000 morning-after pills each year to girls under 16.

Valerie Riches, director of Family and Youth Concern, warns: "Once you have got the parents out of the way, you have a very vulnerable market, because you have removed the one stabilising factor from their lives."

If the Victorians had done this to their girl-children, we should look back on it with horror and denounce it in politically correct history books as child exploitation. Because we are doing it ourselves, we cannot see the wickedness of it.
28/3/96

In some out-of-the-way seaside resort you may still be able to buy a gently rude postcard called Last Year's Pleasure On Wheels. It shows a young mother propelling a pram, containing a red-faced, howling infant, along some dreary promenade.

She is already bulging with her next child and her scrawny husband cringes beside her with the careworn expression of one who will never have enough beer money again.

Laughing in the background are a sexy, slender young couple who do not yet realise that, in 12 months' time, they too will be tethered to pram, mortgage and overdraft.

Postcards like these date from the days when women still "fell" pregnant, an expression you do not hear very often nowadays because the idea that childbirth is an involuntary tumble into fate does not make much sense.

What with the ordinary Pill, the morning-after pill and easy abortion, you have to kick your way through a series of safety nets before you can possibly have a baby.

But it is not only the awesome bioengineering of the Pill and the neutralising of the ancient fear of killing the unborn which have brought us to this point. Something else has changed in women's hearts. Very few men could ever be persuaded to become fathers by pure reason. But women used to yearn for children in a way their daughters do not seem able to grasp.

Whether you think it is propaganda, enslavement or progress, it is obvious that the idea of career success has displaced the urge for motherhood among our more successful and intelligent young females.

Mintel's perceptive survey of the young, released this week, showed that up to one in five of today's 20–34-year-olds could remain childless throughout their lives. A scary 17 per cent actually declared that they "hope not to have children". Many others are putting off parenthood, a postponement far riskier than they think because new research suggests that infertility begins much earlier than once believed.

This should be no great surprise. Today's young have seen the sadness of their own mothers who gave up work for parenthood and ended up in empty nests. They have seen the failure of the superwoman myth, and will have read last week's miserable revelations about "opulent neglect" by double-job, double-income parents who can give their offspring everything except their time.

The taboos have also come off once-forbidden subjects, from the pain of childbirth to the chores of nappy-changing, the broken sleep, the domestic mess, the winged hell of family holidays and the colossal cost of raising one new human being from cradle to maturity.

Behind that lies the knowledge that lifetime jobs no longer exist, and that the one-breadwinner household is practically extinct. Meanwhile, the old network of unpaid advisers and babysitters known as the extended family has shrivelled and died as we scatter ourselves across the land.

If this – loneliness, mess and poverty – is the price of responsibility, then the brightest and the best and the smartest are going to avoid it.

In a grotesque paradox, parenthood has become popular at exactly the same time among the feckless and unsettled, who have discovered that a baby is a ticket to perpetual low-grade security.

And young, uneducated men with no chance of career achievement take a pride in fatherhood which would make perfect sense to a Viking chieftain in the dark ages but which would baffle a twenty-something solicitor or bond trader.

Sadly, the melting away of the marriage bond means that these young men's pride rarely leads on – as it would once have done – to responsibility and maturity. We have made it easy for them to run away. In fact, we have made it too easy for all of us to run away. On a rational accounting, hardly anyone would be willing to enter into parenthood.

One of the strongest arguments for a intelligent creator is that procreation follows on from pleasure. Another is that children teach us unselfishness and force us into maturity as nothing else can. From the first moment of parenthood, a couple find themselves more carefully chaperoned and watched than if they had brought a rather traditionalist nun to live in their home.

Unpleasant behaviour is mimicked and caricatured, rude words copied, kindness, patience and affection rewarded. Becoming an exemplar to a two-year-old is an astonishingly fast route to self-knowledge.

For the first time in their lives, new parents are literally forced to consider other people before themselves. In some ways more vital still, they must begin to worry about a wider society. They can no longer believe, like the economist Maynard Keynes, that "in the long run we are all dead", for they suddenly see that they will probably have grandchildren and must concern themselves about what kind of country they will live in.

So the turn away from parenthood which we now see is not merely a fad or a trend. It is a threat to a stable and happy future for all of us, and a symptom of unease among people who, in many cases, have been brought up not by their work-obsessed parents but by TV.

This has already gone much further in the USA, where contact between teenagers and their mothers and fathers is often limited to a few minutes a week.

The American Robert Bly, author of the pro-male tract *Iron John*, is about to publish a new warning, *The Sibling Society*. He says that this is a "society in which impulse is given its way. People don't bother to grow up and we are all fish swimming in a tank of half-adults."

We feared our fate, dreaded turning into our own parents, fought to escape from what many in the post-war years saw as the narrow prison of home and family. And we have escaped, through ingenuity and through the greatest moral revolution since the Reformation.

Only now, when the kissing has to stop and the wine bars close and the credit cards go over the limit do we discover that outside the prison walls lies a howling, empty wilderness of purposeless pleasure and endless adolescence.

6/6/96

Why sex lessons are ruining the age of innocence

There is something more than a little creepy about people who actually *want* to tell children about sex, given that most adults naturally shrink from the task.

Yet we have been persuaded to give these characters a free pass into our schools, and so into the minds of our young, by a ruthlessly co-ordinated propaganda campaign.

The message, pounded into our heads by constant repetition, is that our daughters will get pregnant and our sons will contract awful diseases because they are ignorant of the facts of life.

Of course, we do not want this to happen. We would be quite inhuman if we were not frightened by such stories. And, propelled by fear down the path of mass sex education, parents gradually surrender more and more control over this part of their children's lives.

We reluctantly abandon long-held and perfectly reasonable beliefs about morality, propriety, privacy and decorum and soon begin shamefacedly to suppress our own doubts.

Like defendants at some awful show trial, we recant everything we were brought up to believe and confess to having been "prejudiced" in the past. Having now become "enlightened", we are ready to accept whatever the sex education lobby wishes to introduce into the nation's classrooms.

The advance of sex education has been relentless since it first arrived in schools a generation ago. Its results have been, at best, dubious. And there are many who would regard its introduction as a disaster. Yet the lobbyists have been masterly in presenting every failure as either non-existent or, more often, as the fault of someone else. Thus we find ourselves in the current position, where unsuccessful sex educationists blame their shortcomings on the lack of sex education.

As an example of the way they have been betrayed, they point to the experience of Holland, where sex education flows like water and has resulted in a huge decrease in unwanted teenage pregnancy.

Like all skilled exponents of propaganda, they overlook certain salient points – most notably that the age of sexual consent in Holland is 12, and that some forms of abortion, including the widely used morning-after pill, are excluded from the figures. This pill, despite its potent effects on the human frame, is now being used more and more in Britain as well and may already have led to a drop in our own teenage conception totals – though the sex education campaigners will almost certainly claim the credit for themselves.

They have little right to do so. Since the mid-Seventies, as the network of birth control clinics and sex educators has fanned out across the country, abortion has grown steadily in almost every year but one. That year – 1985 – followed Victoria Gillick's short-lived Appeal Court victory, when the judges ruled that girls under 16 could not be given contraceptives without their parents' permission. Once the House of Lords overturned the Gillick ruling, the queues at the condom clinics instantly lengthened again and – in a paradox which makes nonsense of the sex educators' propaganda – the abortion figures resumed their tragic upward march.

Despite this, and despite the fact that there cannot now be anyone in Britain over the age of 11 who does not know how babies are made, the sex education industry continues to press for access to younger and younger minds, and for the right to act without parental consent.

The truth is that the problem is not – yet – anything like as big as they claim it is. Nor is Britain "lagging behind" other countries in enlightenment. If playground drug abuse were as rare as under-age pregnancy we could be quite pleased with ourselves.

But it does not suit the sex propagandists to admit that. They need constant national unease so that they can push their way into the schools with their "value-free" information packs of rubber goods and artificial penises.

And, of course, they are value-free. That is the whole point of them. They portray sex as mechanical recreation, without consideration, commitment or faithful marriage. They loathe and mock the idea that it does *and should* lead to responsible joint parenthood.

Perhaps worst of all, they open a deep breach between parent and child by creating a zone of secrecy and lies, in which other lies, perhaps about drugs and theft, can grow.

The fatherly talk to a son about "birds and bees" may have been excruciatingly embarrassing, as was a mother's wedding eve chat with her daughter. But each served its purpose and retained in society an understanding of the link between love and sex.

Every civilisation before ours has surrounded sex with taboos, limits and ceremonies because of its power to move us – and because it is inseparably linked to fertility. Our ancestors strove for centuries to protect the young from sexual exploitation, because they knew that every child needed a period of innocence and trust, in which it could grow to maturity.

How is it that we, products of the century which gave us germ warfare, the concentration camp, the tower-block, the traffic jam, and epidemic divorce, think we know better?

25/2/97

PC

What a creepy country this is becoming. I seem to be living in what Tony Blair might call "The People's Dictatorship".

Certain thoughts are getting harder and harder to express in the open. Publishers, broadcasters and others are acting as if there is a single "People's Opinion" which alone has the right to be spoken aloud. The feeling that freedom of speech was menaced grew rapidly after the death of Princess Diana. We lived beneath a tyranny of grief, when millions of people were forced to hide their true views.

Last week I met a man who was denounced to his employer by a passer-by who overheard him say that the mourning was exaggerated.

But the repressive mood has not faded since. Leaders of opinion queue to suck up to Labour in power and supposedly bold satirists jeer at the impotent Tories, like schoolboys poking sticks through the bars at a dying tiger and praising themselves for their bravery.

It is now conventional wisdom among commentators that William Hague made a blunder when he attacked Tony Blair for hijacking the funeral. Conventional wisdom, as usual, is wrong. Millions loathed Mr Blair's stagey reading of the lesson in Westminster Abbey and still resent the fact that he was there at all.

And millions believe that the Prime Minister squeezed advantage from the Princess's death. In fact, Diana herself predicted it, weeks before she died. She told Tina Brown, of *The New Yorker* magazine: "I think at last I have someone who will know how to use me." She was referring to Mr Blair, though she can have had no idea how truly she spoke.

But these millions are still voiceless. This week's Labour Party conference will be used to strengthen the idea that Britain is somehow besotted by Mr Blair and in love with his government.

Will the delegates wave little Union Jacks to celebrate the break-up of the UK? Will doves of peace descend from the ceiling and alight on Mr Blair's shoulders? Will there be hushed reverence from the impartial BBC? Will Mr Blair's speech be praised as if he were a combination of Winston Churchill and Laurence Olivier?

As a known dissident, I have been given the lowliest possible grade of conference Press pass and will probably not be allowed in the hall during the Dear Leader's Great Speech, owing to the need to find seats for cooing sycophants. Even so, I will try to give you a cooler version of events next week.
29/9/97

A top class system for fostering brilliance

I like the English class system. Among my recent ancestors are a Wiltshire farm labourer and a Polish Jewish immigrant pedlar and I don't think my origins have held me back all that much. In fact, I'm proud of both sides.

And yet this hugely subtle and complex structure of accents, manners, tastes and loyalties has – I'm sure – helped me and millions of others. How?

Put simply, we have always known where and who we were and how we fitted into the national family. Even new arrivals have quickly discovered how to become English, once they have decided what sort of English men and women they wish to be.

Peter Bauer, now an English Lord, is the immigrant son of a Hungarian bookie and rightly recognises the wonderful flexibility of our society, which has always encouraged talent. And this week he has published a pamphlet, Class on the Brain, which debunks the silly idea that this is a country where fusty snobbery holds back brilliance.

Personally, I have seen very little snobbery from those with real rank and much more from those near the bottom of the pyramid, desperate to maintain a status they value more highly than money.

Class also softens the naked power of riches and ambition. In England – certainly until recently – class insisted that wealth and power should clothe themselves in good manners and gentleness and prized a man's honour and good name far above the thickness of his bank book.

The classless society, as we now find, rewards the ruthless and the rude. It also grovels to power. Which is why socialist states grade their citizens far more harshly than the English ever did.

29/9/97

Driven to kill

Each year this country makes and exports tens of thousands of devices which kill and maim children all over the world. Even more shockingly, we import them from Japan, Italy, France and Germany and they are on open sale in many High Streets.

By passing a simple test, almost anyone can get hold of one of these deadly contraptions. Yet because huge corporations make profits from them and governments are too cowardly to halt their manufacture, their numbers grow each year. The penalties for killing a child with one of these things are pitifully weak.

They are called motor cars. Once we have got over our emotional spasm about landmines, how about a worldwide ban on these far more fearsome weapons of destruction.
6/10/97

Monuments to principle

I always try to stop and look at war memorials. It is the least I can do for those whose names are carved upon them, given what they did for me.

Surprisingly often, I find my own not-very-common surname among the dead, and feel a cold fingertip touch my spine.

This week I came upon a rather fierce monument near Blackpool which declared: "Principles do not apply themselves."

This seems rather a good motto. Those Tories who have now decided that marriage does not matter might take note of it. When our most treasured values are threatened, people must stand up for them. Sometimes, they will have to risk bullets to do so. Sometimes they will merely have to risk a little unpopularity.

What Michael Portillo seemed to be saying last week was that Tories shouldn't fight for lifelong marriage because it was currently out of fashion.

I can only give thanks that the young men of 1914 and 1939 did not have such a light-minded approach to defending all that we have and are.

15/12/97

Are the Simpsons looking after your children?

If you *will* leave your children in the care of a stranger, then don't be surprised. No, this is not a reference to the au pair whose plight has entangled the nation in yellow ribbons, but to the television set you may well have installed in your child's bedroom.

The absurd and feeble Broadcasting Standards Council is complaining that the BBC and ITV have packed their children's schedules with cartoons.

Well, what a surprise. The unspoken secret of this decade is that one of the main roles of TV is to provide a free national child-minding service.

If children don't have TV sets in their own rooms, then they have mastery of the family set and the remote control, usually until way past the comical nine o'clock watershed.

Today's adults shamelessly use the flickering, braying, never-silent device to mesmerise the next generation, so that they can get on with their grown-up lives.

We can't let them play outside in case they get erased by teenage drivers, cruising the suburbs at 50 mph in overpowered cars. Alternatively, we can't let them go off to the park on their own in case a podgy paedophile is haunting the swings.

We're too tired to talk to them or read to them, the poor things can themselves barely read anyway. They mostly see it as an archaic and baffling activity, like handloom-weaving or petit-point, which they are occasionally forced to tackle at school but expect to escape from at home.

So it's the TV: cost-free, effort-free, almost always there, especially early on Sunday mornings when wageslave mother and wageslave father alike can slumber on.

This, by the way, is how millions of parents discovered so early in the day that Princess Diana was dead. The children switched on their electronic dripfeeds and instead of wall-to-wall cartoon drivel, they got wall-to-wall Diana news.

And of course they rushed upstairs to complain to the authorities, who quickly discovered that, just this once the TV stations were providing nothing but the factual programmes that the Broadcasting Standards Council like so much.

Actually, such programmes would not do the job. "The broadcast media form an integral part of the development of today's child," says the BBC chairman, Lady Howe. "Quality programming for children should encourage the child's development as a good citizen with critical abilities and an interest in a wide range of issues."

Ha, ha. Poor Lady Howe seems to be dwelling still in a Britain of detachable collars, galoshes, coalsheds, solid puddings and Sir Stafford Cripps – the skeletal Chancellor of the Exchequer who delighted in austerity.

What she and the commission fail to understand is that TV cartoons are the screen equivalent of cheeseburgers, french fries and ice cream, while the programmes she likes are electronic steamed fish, spinach and broccoli.

Just as you have to stand over a child to get him to consume foods that are good for him, you have to sit with him to get him to watch programmes that are good for him. But that would defeat the whole purpose of the bedroom set, to be the third parent.

So children do not laze in front of cartoons to be informed or turned into responsible citizens. They watch *The Simpsons*, *Rugrats*, *Attack of the Killer Tomatoes*, and the rest of them because they require no effort, no imagination and no knowledge – apart from a few quickly acquired in-jokes and catchphrases.

They may not actually know for certain that they have been dumped but they sense that what they are expected to do is to slump. They require a TV diet that is, above all, not actively boring or difficult, with plenty of colour, noise, action and simple plotting.

They haven't the slightest desire to be informed or made responsible. What is more the TV stations have not the money or the will to do this, even if children would be willing to watch it.

It is expensive to make the "superb nature programmes" with which TV executives and parents alike salve their consciences, rightly guilt-ridden over the slurry that spreads across so much television – which the companies make and parents allow their young to watch.

If a single, puritan, collar-and-tie channel still broadcast an hour of children's TV a day, and then closed down until the evening, it might be possible for that one hour to be all Lady Howe desires: instructive, literate, moral.

But such things could only happen in the days when society controlled television. Now television more or less controls society, shapes its tastes and sets its trends.

We live with five Earthbound channels broadcasting almost without a break, and an endlessly breeding number of cable and satellite stations in a world where TV is unquestionably the dominant medium. Lady Howe's plea is just fantasy.

Why learn to be an active questioning individual when it is both pleasurable and easy to be passive and conformist? Even *Blue Peter* now looks as if its cast hopes to be auditioned by MTV.

Why insist that children's TV should have a moral or educational purpose when you allow – without controversy – the showing of sick pornography like Quentin Tarantino's *Pulp Fiction* on a mainstream channel?

In far too many areas of life we blame governments and authorities, even TV stations, for doing pretty much what we want them to do. If we would only bring up our own children ourselves – hard work though it is – we would need neither the cartoons to pacify our young, nor Lady Howe's redundant preaching to tell us that it was wrong.

6/11/97

I have a horrible picture fixed in my mind. It is of a boy, aged about 12, crouched over a computer game machine in a French cafe, with a pile of coins at his elbow and a cigarette burning in the corner of his mouth.

His face is pale and blank as you might imagine the face of an assassin or a slave. It is strangely wizened and creased, like that of an old man and yet also terribly young. Even his hair is lifeless. The sight made me want to vomit and darkened the entire day.

From that moment around 10 years ago, I have been unshakeably opposed to children playing computer games, which are even more destructive of thought and imagination than television.

Other parents have claimed that these things are educational and that having a computer in the house is essential. Teachers often assume that their pupils have access to such a machine at home. Politicians boast of plans to equip schools with them.

Be suspicious of this. Most home computers are used to play games, which are often perverse and sick and which invariably drag the player out of the real world into a place of fantasy where he becomes far more important and powerful.

The young Adolf Hitler, one senses, would have loved this. Imagine the sort of games he would have devised.

Apart from the increasingly popular *Tomb Raider* featuring the schoolboy fantasy breasts of heroine Lara Croft, many of the best-selling games are brutal or even bloody.

One, based on *Jurassic Park*, features humans being eaten by dinosaurs as blood splashes and screams echo.

Another, which may explain why so many under-25s drive like drugged gangsters, is called *Carmaggedon*. The player has to run over as many people as possible, including children. The victims let out screams and spit blood as they die.

The game can be "enhanced" so that severed heads roll across your windscreen and limbs fly across the road.

People who use these things confess that they often take some time to come down afterwards, and think of the real world as if it is part of the game.

I know, from personal experience of famines and carnage, that I have myself been desensitised by TV pictures of hunger and massacre and was unable to feel the full horror of them when I met them face to face.

I do not call for this electronic slurry to be banned. There would only be a black market. But I urge parents to realise the sort of thing their children are watching alone in their bedrooms.

My advice remains: if you would not let your sons and daughters drink gin or smoke opium, you should keep them away from unsupervised TV sets and computers.

22/9/97

Shame of the silly sisters

Last night there was a modish gathering in London to commemorate the life and death of Jessica Mitford.

Among those taking part were my left-wing brother Christopher and the lofty C4 newsreader Jon Snow who once called me a "Hitlerite" because I failed to agree with him about nuclear disarmament.

Jessica Mitford was one of the silliest members of a very odd family. She became a communist in the Thirties, at least partly to spite her equally silly sister, Unity, who became a Nazi. Both of them, I suspect, thought they were playing some sort of nursery game.

They weren't, of course. Unity's friend Hitler was the modern world's second-worst mass murderer. If you held a commemoration of her in a London theatre, people would quite rightly stay away.

Jessica's Soviet friends murdered even more people and carried on doing it until quite recently. Yet we are not supposed to despise her for her past. Why do we indulge and pardon one set of fellow-travellers while turning a cold shoulder to the other lot?

In fairness why should we ever forgive either of these troops of fools and dupes? Does Jessica Mitford escape because she wrote a couple of funny books? Would Unity have cleared her name by doing the same?

12/2/97

Every time I see a cartoon of a dove of peace, I reach for my cookery book. Pigeon (or dove) with steak and stout makes an excellent pie, tastefully garnished with a little olive branch. The dove and the olive branch in the Bible have nothing to do with peace at all. They were merely a sign to Noah that the flood was receding and there was dry land again (Genesis Chapter 8, Verse 11). So where does this stupid, soppy cartoon fowl come from?

1/6/98

Culture

People are beginning to dread old age in a way not known since the days of the workhouse. The reality affects both young and old, for those now in their prime are having to watch as their parents face death with indignity.

It is not just the cruel stripping away of savings to pay for nursing care. It is the creeping fear that our last days on earth will be a hell of misery, neglect and pain.

A reader has sent me an account of the death of her 82-year-old mother, Elizabeth, in a London hospital during April. It is brief and terrible.

Elizabeth, like so many old people nowadays, had been active and spry until her final days. First she waited four hours to be seen by a doctor who sent her home with painkillers.

The pain grew 10 times worse. Her daughter called an "emergency" doctor, and was told there was a two hour wait for his services.

Nearly three hours later, there was no doctor, and she was told there was now a six hour wait. Sensing her mother was dying, the daughter abandoned hopes of keeping her at home because the pain was so bad. She dialled 999.

Ambulancemen arrived swiftly, proof that at least one part of the NHS still works properly. They were shocked that the old lady had been sent home in the first place.

Elizabeth's daughter says: "I really thought that as she had come into hospital as an emergency she would be seen quickly, but only one or two nurses came to do routine things. I told everyone I saw that she was in great pain, but nobody seemed to listen to what I was saying."

She buttonholed a doctor who was too anxious to go off duty to see her. "Perhaps my mother should have been screaming by now, but her voice was nearly gone and she could only whisper."

Ages later, another doctor appeared, but he could not think of anything suitable to give her – and she was sent home again at 3 am. While Elizabeth waited in the crowded, chaotic casualty department for a minicab to take her home, she was probably in too much pain to notice the feral teenagers, making fun of her, a sick bewildered lady in nightie and fluffy bedsocks. In our youth obsessed age they did not understand that she was once as young as they, and they too will one day be old and weak. "She could not stand, let alone, walk, so I had to leave her clinging to the banister while I paid the minicab driver," Elizabeth's daughter recalls.

The description of her final day is too harrowing and pitiful and personal, for me to repeat it here. Her daughter says: "We do not live in a Third World country but in Greater London. I was surrounded by millions of people, but no one would help. All I came across was indifference."

No amount of money could have prevented this. For far too long we have thought that science, drugs and cash were substitutes for human kindness and generosity. They are not. The sickness in our society is not the result of Lady

Thatcher's nonexistent "cuts", but of our selfishness as a people.

1/6/98

Traditions: our future depends upon them

Tony Blair's best friend hates being made to wear black stockings and a wig. He is the Lord Chancellor, Lord Irvine, whose job requires him to don these items and a superb cloak heavy with gold thread.

Derry, as he likes to be called, would prefer to go to court in a plain black cotton Euro-robe, a "People's Judge". He objects to his 17th-century costume, calling it "old-fashioned, out of touch and self-satisfied".

This sort of boring modernity is itself old-fashioned Sixties stuff. We used to hear it then from those obsessed with making everything "up-to-date". Their trendy changes, of course, looked tired and worn out within five years.

Yet it is significant, part of a broad attack by this Government on the traditions and customs of this country.

The Minister without Portfolio, Mr Peter Mandelson, is urging Britain to become a nation without a memory. We should, he suggests, seek our identity not in the past but in the future.

Since we cannot possibly know the future, he is asking for a national act of amnesia. Mr Mandelson and Lord Irvine want us to make a pyre of our memories.

Why is this? Why do they see our history as a burden? Why did they hold the Anglo-French summit in a tower-block that looks as if it is made of plastic and has escaped from Houston?

Instead, they could have conferred in any one of a hundred glorious and civilised buildings, which sing and hum with our amazing story of adventure, justice and freedom.

I think it is because they wish to be children of their own

time. They think, as revolutionaries always do, that they know better.

To accept tradition is to grasp that we are civilised only because we stand on the shoulders of others.

Those who reject it are like a silly couple who buy an old house, knock down a load-bearing wall and then gape in amazement when the building crashes about their ears.

Tradition warns that the world does not belong to us but that we hold it in trust – inherited from the dead and destined for the unborn.

Tradition spares us from having to go through all the hard lessons of life ourselves. We have no need of flogging or the pillory or the workhouse because our forefathers suffered these things and learned from them. But if we ignore their experience and cast it to one side, then we are doomed to repeat the miseries of the past, or something even worse.

Tradition is the experience we do not have to undergo, the battle we do not have to fight, the war we do not have to win, the betrayal we do not need to suffer. It does not belong to Derry Irvine or to Peter Mandelson. And it tends to take revenge on those who sneer at it.

10/11/97

Don't care

The Prime Minister has censored the word "Christmas" from the cards he has sent to non-Christians abroad. I hope he does not do this again.

It reminds me of the sad USA, where nobody now dares say "Merry Christmas" any more, and everyone has to mumble "Happy Holidays" instead.

Thanks to this, despite the elaborate decorations and the much more seasonal weather of Washington DC, Christmas Eve and Christmas Day felt curiously flat and meaningless there.

We had better Christmases in officially atheist Moscow, where the whole mighty feast had to be contained within the walls of our flat, while the great city outside carried on unmoved.

I sense that the Premier's neutered greetings card is influenced by the ghastly new conformism, which wrongly fears that the world's other faiths will be upset or angered by the greatest season of the year.

This is the same spirit that teaches religion in schools as a sort of curiosity to be studied and then avoided, unless it is someone else's. Do a project on Christmas, but treat it as a curious survival, not the heart of your civilisation. That might upset the others whose festivals often get more sympathetic treatment than Christian feasts.

How feeble. I do not believe that the true follower of any faith is offended by the honest expression of another one.

When the ticket collector on my train proudly told me that he had finally made the pilgrimage to Mecca, one of the great goals of his life, I shook his hand with admiration and some envy.

I am glad to receive New Year cards from Jewish relatives and friends, and to attend their celebrations. They are, in the Pope's fine words, the elder brothers of our faith.

What I fear, in this time of paganism and selfishness, is the empty indifference and hollow pleasure of a festival without any meaning at all except to mark the invention of television.

Happy Christmas to all of you.

22/12/97

At a church in my home town, they lost the key to the cupboard where the service books were kept.

They tried to manage without the books, stumbling through their devotions from memory. Yet, though they had been saying the new version of the Our Father for years, nobody could remember it.

"Let's say the old one," somebody piped up. Everyone knew it by heart.

Of course they did. Like all the old prayers, it was written by men whose lives were filled with poetry and music, chanted among echoing stone arches.

They knew the secret rhythms of language without being told. And they knew that nine tenths of the point of prayers is that you will be able to remember them when, frightened and alone, you suddenly find you need them after all.

16/2/98

Mountain king's wise TV ban is example to West

As Prince Charles toured the lovely and mysterious kingdom of Bhutan, TV commentators could barely believe that television is banned there. Why? It is an enormous pity that more countries did not hesitate before allowing this dangerous and revolutionary invention to invade their societies.

If TV were a drug or a new medical treatment, it would certainly be forbidden in many places, and available only under strict licence in others.

Yet we, who can ban beef on the bone and frighten people away from aspirin with panic tales of internal bleeding, cheerfully expose tiny children to TV.

One day, in a world gone utterly mad, Bhutan may be the place from which the rebuilding of civilisation begins. A people without TV still have imagination, still know how to think for themselves and to speak to each other. Their senses are not dulled, they are not slaves to each new conformist fashion. Long may the King of Bhutan maintain his wise policy.*

16/2/98

What is the point of the Church of England? It would be easier to answer this question if I asked what *isn't* the point of

_____

*He didn't

59

it. Perhaps we would realise why we needed this kindly, strangely influential yet decrepit old ruin, if it were swept away and replaced by its opposite, a National Church of Self, which preached that violence, wife-beating, divorce, abortion, homosexuality, theft, drug-taking, child abuse, fraud and cheating were not only right, but desirable goals for all.

Each Sunday, in ugly modern buildings pulsing with the sexual beat of rock music, its hard-faced flock could gather – sometimes to watch a pornographic video, sometimes to share some narcotics or an unnatural erotic act, sometimes to sell some stolen goods to one another as a "sign of peace".

It would also have ceremonies where everyone would gather round and urge pregnant young women to kill their unborn babies, or tell divorcing parents that they were "doing the right thing" and "sparing their children a lot of pain". It would encourage same-sex couples to take part in a sick caricature of marriage.

I fear that such a church would quickly gain a lot of support from modern society. It would certainly fit in with the supposed desires of a lot of "young people", poor conformist wimps scared to stand up against the moral garbage fed to them by TV stations and the rock business.

But would that make it right? Of course not. If there is one thing we know for certain from this grisly century, it is that the majority are usually wrong and that today's fashion is tomorrow's embarrassment and even shame. So where is a proper church to take its teachings from, if not from market research, focus groups and opinion polls?

Why, where they always came from, of course. From the great scriptures and gospels, from the beliefs which sustained our ancestors through times so hard we cannot even imagine them and which inspired them to create the greatest music, write the finest poetry and raise the loveliest buildings the world has ever known. Some in the Church of England understand this. But many do not. They have sought cheap popularity and short-term gain by pandering to the worship of youth, by trying to do a deal with the 20th century.

It cannot be. People yearn for someone, anyone, to swim against the tide of ethical effluent which sweeps through our lives. They feel dispirited and abandoned when they see their leaders faltering. They cannot understand why those who defy the gospels are allowed to become and remain ministers of religion.

If the English bishops had shown half the guts of their brothers in Africa, by standing up for what is eternally right then they would not be jokes in purple dressing gowns, but the respected generals of an army with banners.

26/6/96

Sorry about the apology on Platform 1

My railway station surpassed its annual target for apologies this week, thanks to a computerised voice which is programmed to say "sorry" in an appealing feminine tone, giving a variety of excuses.

Occasionally it oversteps itself and a gruff real voice breaks in on the loudspeaker system to say "Will passengers please ignore the previous apology, which was totally wrong. Your train is not in fact being held up by escaped giraffes on the line but by a lorry stuck under a bridge."

The gruff voice then apologises again for calling us passengers instead of customers and sets everyone scuttling up and down the platform with a favourite game telling us that the train is in "reverse order" and that the sub-standard class is now at the front instead of the back, where it usually is. When the train arrives – delayed but the right way round – this provides the pretext for a further apology, as we mill about like crazed worker ants.

Is a computerised apology real? How many times is someone allowed to say "sorry" for doing the same thing over and over again?

Years ago, someone told the railways it was time they apologised a bit more. Since then, it seems, they have been doing little else. But have they missed the point?

2/11/98

A textbook way to define bias

Young people are seldom Tories. A Tory is a socialist who has discovered how much tax he is paying and how little he is getting for it – something under-25s generally haven't found out yet. But there is something alarming in the complete collapse of conservative loyalties among the young shown in last week's survey of Britain's youth.

Personally, I blame the cultural revolution in schools, in broadcasting, in comedy, in entertainment. It's amazing how deep it has gone. These fields seem to be dominated by people who don't even know they're biased. A reader e-mailed me with these definitions from a Chambers school dictionary: "The Labour Party – one of the chief political parties of Great Britain, which has the aim of representing the working people and achieving greater social equality." The description of the Liberal-Democrats is similar but turn to "Conservative" and what do you get?

"A Right-wing political party in the UK."

If you then go on to look up the entries for fascism and communism, you find that communism is just about nationalisation of industry while fascism is correctly identified as a threat to individual liberty.

Dictionaries are supposed to provide facts, not opinions, and Chambers say they will be revising the references in future editions. But they insist: "We must stress that these entries do not reflect a political bias on the part of the editors or the company."

Well, what *do* they reflect, then? I can only urge you to look very carefully at dictionaries and encyclopaedias intended for the young.

16/1/98

Go on, admit that Mary Whitehouse was right

That queen of knee-jerk leftism Polly Toynbee complains that our world is obsessed with sex. She whines about "freak shows, sexologists and fatuous innuendoes". She doesn't like the "cheap and mindless sexualisation of everything around us". Just a moment, Polly. Wasn't it your liberal pals who wanted all this? Wasn't it your side who said *Lady Chatterley's Lover* – one of D.H. Lawrence's worst books – was such a shining piece of literature that it should go on open sale despite its tawdry sex and bad language? Didn't your lot queue up to defend the poisonous, grunting filth of *Last Exit To Brooklyn*, claiming it was the equal of George Eliot and Charles Dickens?

Didn't they say that the smut and porno cartoons of schoolkids' *Oz* were a blow for liberty? Didn't they mock saintly Mary Whitehouse, who defied your jeers with the sort of quiet courage Britain used to be famous for?

Well, you got your liberty and it's just as bad as Mrs Whitehouse said it would be. You can either apologise for being wrong and help me put the clock back or learn to like the nasty world you helped to make. You can't have it both ways.

7/12/98

Why Red Nose Day bullies make me see red

I hate Red Nose Day and Comic Relief. There, now I've said it. I loathe the whole idea that rock stars and self-styled "comedians" have any right to bully you and me into giving money to charities of their choice. I am offended by the highly publicised merit they seem to expect.

Hasn't anybody told them that true charity is done in secret? Giving and raising money is not actually much of a good deed. As William Blake said, if you wish to do good to your fellow-man, you must do it in minute particulars.

The old-fashioned kindness and good manners we used to show to each other were worth more than a thousand painless credit card donations. I also dislike the slight sense of compulsion, the vague but insistent feeling that you are not quite the right sort of person if you don't take part, reinforced by the way children are used to dragoon their parents into the wretched thing. It reminds me, ever so faintly, of Communist May Days in the years of the Warsaw Pact, when everyone had to turn out for the parade, cheer the tanks and rockets and stick a little red nose – sorry, flag – on their balconies. It wasn't against the law to abstain but it was noticed, if you know what I mean.
15/3/99

I watched the eclipse on a favourite hillside near my home, in the alleged 97 per cent area. Along with hundreds of others at the same spot, I was left muttering: "Is that it?", after a brief period of mild dusk. Birds continued to fly, petals remained open, and an irritating dog barked before, during and afterwards.

I turned to go, along a tree-shaded lane. There was something odd about the dappled patterns on the road. I suddenly realised that each one of the thousands of shadows was a tiny crescent. It was most moving, like finding myself on the surface of a different planet where everything was subtly different from the familiar.

To me, the most enthralling thing about the eclipse was that it happens at all. The supposed coincidence of the moon's size and its distance from the sun is so incredibly unlikely that I don't believe it is a coincidence at all. In which case it's part of a design, in which case...
16/8/99

Why is marriage the word they won't use?

If the schools gave driving lessons to nine-year-olds would you be surprised if there was a sharp increase in the amount of underage motoring not to mention fatal crashes and car theft? Wouldn't things be even worse if they taught them how to start and steer a car, but not how to stop it?

And what if the teachers didn't mention the Highway Code or the Road Traffic Acts, so that these tots were sent out on the road with no knowledge of what a red light meant?

Any council which did anything so stupid would be laughed out of office.

Yet the arguments used for sex education in the primary schools, where it now often begins, could also be used for teaching motorway skills to classes of mixed infants – while keeping them in ignorance of the rules of the road.

After all we live in a society where almost everyone drives. Driving is widely accepted as the only way of getting around. People talk about it all the time. You see it on the TV and in the movies, where it is portrayed as being much more exciting than it really is.

Done badly, it can have terrible consequences. Parents are often rather clumsy at explaining its finer points to their own children.

There's one other similarity. It's against the law to do it until a fixed age is reached, for the very good reason that children are not thought to be wise and mature enough to attempt anything so risky and responsible. Just like sex.

The 14-year-old boy in Sheffield who claims to have had a harem of tiny paramours, and has now got a 12-year-old with child, learned how to have sex at school years before it was legal for him to do so. But, along with millions of others, he wasn't told why people do it or when to do it. He certainly didn't learn when not to do it.

And for once we can be sure that this wasn't because his

teachers were blundering incompetents. It was because the "sex education" handed out in our schools is a stream of unfeeling information, all technique, safety warnings and no morals.

A cynic, as we all think we know, is someone who knows the price of everything and the value of nothing. There could be no more perfect example of this than "sex education", which almost never mentions that forbidden word "marriage". It treats sex as a hobby or a game, divorced from commitment, true joy or parenthood.

In a survey of local authority sex education guides for the excellent Family Education Trust in Oxford, Paul Atkin found that "all sex education guides studied were implicitly hostile to the view that the two-parent family based on marriage was the best possible place for children to grow and develop. Writers of many syllabuses go to imaginative and often ridiculous lengths to avoid references to traditional family life."

In one county's "ABC of sex education" bisexuality, homosexuality, fetishism, lesbianism, masturbation and pornography all feature. Chastity, fidelity, right and wrong do not.

This is not education. It is propaganda for the post-marriage society that our new liberal establishment seems so keen on. Princess Tony's moral crusade will do nothing to put this right. Curfews? The law backs teenagers against their parents. And you will wait a hundred years before you hear him saying clearly that he thinks it is better for parents to be married than unmarried.

The M-word hardly ever passes his lips and his government has quietly abolished the last pitiful traces of the privileges which once helped prop up the difficult but honourable estate of marriage, the best guardian of morality and childhood innocence known to man.

6/9/99

If divorce is OK, why not do it in church?

Why doesn't the Church of England just go the whole way and start offering divorce services? If it is so anxious to fit in with the spirit of our times, then I should have thought this would be a pretty good way of doing it.

There could even be all kinds of exciting options, along the lines of the "will the bride agree to obey?" controversy.

Will the ex-husband thrust his ex-wife back into the hands of her disgruntled father, along with a cheque to cover the costs of the now-wasted reception? Or will he pass her direct to her new "partner" (male or female, optional)? Will there be a Worst Man to stand beside his newly-free pal?

Will she throw the ring at him or keep it? Will she get the title deeds of the family house before or afterwards? Will the children sit on the ex-husband's side or the ex-wife's? And so on. The choir could sing "Please release me, let me go". Or preferably not.

Yes, I know it sounds silly. But a lot of what goes on in churches these days is pretty witless. And if vicars and bishops really can't see what's wrong with marrying divorced people in church – which they are now allowing in increasing numbers – then they don't understand what they are for.

Christian marriage has always been for life. It was specially designed to protect women from being tossed aside as they grew older, as well as to ensure the nurture of children and the care of the old.

The founder of the faith said himself: "Those whom God hath joined together, let no man put asunder." I should say that was pretty clear, even to the most modish parson.

This is nothing to do with being censorious about people who divorce. All decent people are grieved by the break-up of a marriage, which diminishes each of us and smashes down one of the pillars of civilisation. But we know that in today's anti-marriage society it is increasingly difficult to last the course.

Those who try against all the odds to keep their vows need all the support they can get.

When government, schools, tax laws, benefits systems, lawyers, pension rules, soap operas, film stars, princes and princesses cannot stand up for marriage, or when they actively attack it, the Church has a fierce duty to defend a bond which it invented, and which is one of its own buttresses.

27/9/99

DRUGS

On the way back to Gin Lane – but does anyone care?

If anything will wake us from our national stupor of selfish complacency, the discovery of an eight-year-old heroin addict, surrounded by used needles, in the suburbs of Blackpool ought to do so.

A sane country would see this as a sign and a warning that it had lost control of itself. Not just because a little child has been corrupted and polluted and poisoned.

Not just because that child's mother and other relatives have foully betrayed the trust placed in them by a defenceless infant, in pursuit of their own repulsive habits.

Nor even because this has taken place in a town once famous for the simple pleasures of the honest poor, whose closest brushes with sin and lies came during the annual conferences of the political parties.

More than all these things, this incident drives home the collapse of the rules which are essential for civilisation to function: responsibility, protection of the weak and innocent by the strong, the trust founded upon this duty, renunciation of selfishness, the vigilance of friends and neighbours.

It should come into our busy lives like a thunderbolt, forcing us to consider the direction and nature of our society, and to resolve to change it rapidly for the better.

But it will not, just as the murder of James Bulger did not, just as the knifing of Philip Lawrence did not, just as the daily and weekly tally of cruelty, ignorance and unkindness all around us do not.

For this, it seems, is how a growing number of us like it. To the unhinged beat of rave music we tread out our moral dance of death, numbed by extra-strong lager or Ecstasy tablets, our imaginations laid waste by televised drivel, certain that we are having a good time.

If we ever woke from this daze of synthetic happiness, in which everything, low-grade, smutty and cheap is elevated to fame and stardom in which Chris Evans and the Gallagher brothers are mistakenly believed to be talented, then we would see that we are dwelling in the ruins of a lost civilisation.

But to criticise this culture of acceptance is to step outside the new normality, which rejects all criticism with gales of laughter – laughter that ought to be reserved for the pathetic political figures who chase popularity by praising "Britpop" as one of the glories of our nation, or accepting the half-wit verdicts of American glossy magazines that London is the coolest place on the planet.

Everything is all right, the kids are all right, the schools are good, the exams are just as tough as they ever were, crime is dropping, children benefit from being abandoned by their mothers, drugs are no different from booze and cigarettes, rock music is as good as J. S. Bach, homosexuals are just as normal as everyone else.

Amid this slurry of weakness and moral relativism, is it surprising that films such as *Trainspotting* – and the book it was based on – are greeted with simpering praise, or that John Travolta was able to rebuild a faltering career on the basis of the movie *Pulp Fiction*?

Is it remotely shocking that the most popular rock band in the country celebrates drug-taking, in its lyrics and in some of its members' lives, or that when its leader is found in possession of cocaine, a timid and morally neutral police force cannot even be bothered to prosecute him?

The police, like the rest of us, have learned to compromise with the new reality because it is so much easier and more pleasant than fighting it.

Listen to Det Sgt John Francis, head of Blackpool police's

drugs unit: "She had probably seen her mother smoking and started to copy her.

"She started doing some tooting or smoking and we have evidence to believe that she also injected it intravenously."

Did you spot it? The use by a senior police officer of junkie jargon – "tooting" – is an important symptom of the collapse of authority. Here we have a tiny defenceless girl smoking a Class A dangerous drug while her sluttish parent looks on smiling, through glazed and narrowed eyes, and the uniformed representative of the law describes the scene by using the soiled language of the underworld.

Even this is nothing like so bad as the attitude of the drug counselling agencies, which all behave as if narcotic abuse were normal, and offer advice on its health risks and effects. They pride themselves on not "preaching".

And yet isn't preaching exactly what we do need? It is almost 250 years since William Hogarth depicted the uglinesss of Gin Lane, another era of deep immorality when parents forgot their duty and poisoned their young.

It was the preaching of John Wesley and his allies, and then the great and determined working–class temperance movements, which eventually freed the poor of this country from the swamps of immorality and selfishness into which they had sunk.

We in the 20th century have forgotten, if we ever knew, how much of our peace, order and civility we owe to our courageous forebears.

And as a people we are never expected to do anything ourselves to put it right. We are encouraged to watch and applaud as SAS troopers are sent to Colombia in pursuit of foreign drug cartels, or the Royal Navy intercepts boatloads of cocaine in the Caribbean, or the self-dramatising hero squads of Customs round up another cargo of pure heroin, etc, etc.

Any day now, no doubt, some police force or other will kit itself out with balaclavas and sledgehammers and stage a series of spectacular raids on the drug businessmen they usually leave well alone, because they know this sort of thing does no real good.

To all those who have helped create this society, a country where heroin is sold openly in once-respectable mining communities; where an entire industry – the rock business – constantly promotes drug use; where self-styled intellectuals call for legalisation of drugs, here is a request:

Please remain silent about the discovery of the nation's first eight-year-old junkie. It is your fault. Pray God the misery you have made never comes near you or yours, and consider, before it is too late, whether your years of sneering at morality and virtue were a mistake.

12/2/97

The dope on dope

As Jack Straw faces a new wave of propaganda claiming that cannabis is cool, here are a few facts to help him swim against the dopehead tide.

The "medical use" argument is phoney. All major medical authorities in the USA reject claims that cannabis is a useful drug, including the American Cancer Society and the US National Multiple Sclerosis Society.

Keith Stroup, a leading campaigner for drug legalisation in the USA, said in 1979: "We will use the medical marijuana argument as a red herring to give pot a good name."

Cannabis can bring on schizophrenia in vulnerable people, and cancel the effects of anti-schizophrenia drugs. The fabled Amsterdam experiment has turned that city into the crime capital of Europe, according to the Dutch Justice Minister (who should know). It has also led to a 250 per cent rise in the use of cannabis by Dutch adolescents, and a 22 per cent increase in the number of registered Dutch hard drug addicts.

Alaska abandoned a flirtation with legalisation after crime, sickness and welfare sponging all went through the roof, as did drug use.

And finally, a firm stand does work. Before Bill Clinton came to the White House, determined campaigning reduced illicit drug users in the USA from 24.3 million citizens in 1979 to 11.4 million in 1992.

5/1/98

We are about to become a society in which drug abuse is considered normal and respectable. The front-line trenches in the real war against narcotics are almost deserted as the enemy prepare their final offensive.

It will succeed mainly because we failed to fight. And after decades of misery, human wreckage and crime that lie ahead, we will have plenty of time to wish we had had more courage.

Just look at the way that so many people have grovelled to the odious Noel Gallagher in the past few days. In a bullying, sneering voice, punctuated by sewer language, this bladder of vanity proclaimed that drug-taking is as normal as having a cup of tea.

Some of the grovellers declared that this was quite true. Others pretended that such words, spoken in such a way, were not an endorsement of the drug culture.

A third group of toadies thanked Mr Gallagher for starting a debate – though the average budgerigar could outsmart this alleged rock genius in any debate involving words of more than four letters.

The usual stage army of failed anti-drug campaigners trundled out their obsolete weapons and dud ammunition ... Ecstasy kills, heroin screws you up, stamp out the evil dealers, blah, blah, blah.

And the Sixties student veterans, who have not had to grow up since they passed the joints round in squalid bedsits, brayed yet again for legalised dope, as if hash-smokers were a persecuted minority.

All this is nonsense, some well-meant, but most self-serving and stupid. Drug-taking is wrong because it is immoral and selfish. Drug dealers would disappear tomorrow if nobody bought their wares.

The Government, the police and the media actively help and encourage the illegal drug industry by treating drugtakers as victims rather than criminals in their own right. They have also granted respectability and immunity to the rock music industry, which promotes drug use with almost every breath it takes.

So why is it immoral? Listen to Allan Bloom's great, pealing denunciation of both drugs and rock in his book *The Closing of the American Mind*: "Rock music provides premature ecstacy and, in this respect, it is like the drugs with which it is allied.

"It artificially induces the exaltation naturally attached to the completion of the greatest endeavours – victory in a just war, consummated love, artistic creation, religious devotion and discovery of the truth. Without effort, without talent, without virtue, anyone and everyone is accorded the equal right to the enjoyment of their fruits.

"Drugs break the natural order, which cleverly connects reward with exertion and sacrifice. Without this link, who will want to work, or even think? Drugs also turn the mind inwards. Who will seek justice and liberty, or strive to build for the future, if happiness is available in a muzzy mental orgasm?"

In this way, the moral heart is poisoned by the act of drug-taking. Robbed of imagination by chemical joy, abusers do not care about the risks because they calculate that they will not be conscious of their own deaths – and so they do not even consider the broken parents and friends left behind.

It is the ultimate selfish pleasure. No wonder so many drugtakers put their enjoyment so high above the rights of others that they become ruthless and merciless thieves as well.

A society in which drugs are as normal as tea will be a terrible place of sloth, cruelty and injustice.

3/2/97

74

Losing our way in a cloud of poison

Soon after the first fox-hunter is sent to jail cannabis will be legal in this country. I do not believe the present Government has any serious objection to dope but I think it hasn't the courage to reveal its true feelings.

What a strange land this will be, when the ancient ritual of the chase is a criminal offence and the sordid solace of the Arab kasbah is on legal sale.

The change will probably be made through a Royal Commission and a private member's Bill and various senior ministers will manage to be absent during the vital debates and votes.

It will be a disaster; Amsterdam, where dope is more or less legal, now, is "the crime capital of Europe" according to the Dutch Justice Minister. Teenage use of cannabis has risen by 250 per cent. The number of registered heroin addicts has grown by a quarter. Organised crime has openly moved in.

Similar miseries happened in Alaska, which did the same thing and then changed its mind after crime, mental illness, welfare spongers and addiction all grew greatly.

Not to mention the other problems. Cannabis can bring on schizophrenia or make it worse. It fries the wiring of the brain, wrecking the imagination and closing the mind. It destroys brain cells far faster than alcohol. Smoked regularly, it is much more cancerous than tobacco, which we are now so busy banning.

Today's cannabis is 10 times as strong as the drug the Sixties generation played with in the age of flower power.

It may, just, be possible for middle-class, well-off, educated people to cope with a dope habit, though I wouldn't recommend it for airline pilots.

But it is already ruining lives on Britain's hundreds of lawless housing estates, where children as young as 12 are regular smokers and steal from their neighbours to pay for their supplies. Its lingering effects are certainly causing a growing number of road deaths.

This is largely because the police, in advance of Parliament, have already given up enforcing the law because it is difficult to do so. Legalisation will end all hope of rescue for the law-abiding and hard-working.

What a price we shall pay so that a few well-off dopeheads, pathetically trying to keep alive the name of youth, can enjoy their selfish pleasure without fear of the courts.

1/12/97

SEXISM

How I will celebrate an awful day for women

Burst those balloons and cancel that parade. Celebrating International Women's Day today is like having a party on Stalin's birthday or Hitler's wedding anniversary.

This day of infamy marks one of the greatest mistakes made by the civilized world this century – the relentless campaign to turn women into wageslaves and *make them think they like it.*

It also commemorates the amazing success, even in free and prosperous countries, of an evil idea beloved by twisted tyrants. No wonder that this sinister holiday has always been kept most keenly in communist states. When I lived in Moscow men were supposed to show they cared today by bestowing bunches of carnations on all the women in their lives.

They were also expecting to do helpful things around the home, and even attempt to cook meals.

Soviet males, perhaps the most spectacular slobs in the history of the planet, seldom fulfilled this particular plan.

Why should they? Since birth the state has seen to it that women did double duty, trudging off to low paid jobs just like their husbands, before going off to hunt and queue for scarce food and stumbling home, dog-tired, to scorch or boil it in tiny kitchens.

In return, it gave them what Western feminists still loudly and stupidly call for, as if they were human rights – abortion on demand and free nurseries where they could dump their children for the working day.

Men were robbed by the state of their role as supporters and protectors, encouraging them to act irresponsibly and without consideration.

Women could have their babies scraped from their wombs in the lunchbreak and then hurry back to their "careers" in exciting places such as the Oil Industry Machinery Construction Ministry.

How else should they all behave? Most Soviet men and women had been brought up by paid strangers beneath portraits of Lenin in depressing kindergartens.

They saw their parents in the evening, and they often saw them drunk, violent and divorced. (The communists made sure divorce was easy, too.)

In some ways, this was understandable in Moscow, a hideous caricature of a city, designed by monsters who hated the family.

They hated the family because it challenged the power of the government and the Communist Party, and they didn't care if they pulled it apart.

How depressing to find that, back in the West, women were actually clamouring for the same sort of life. And getting it.

But here it is capitalism, not communism, doing the dirty work.

Employers like the way that women are often more single-minded and dedicated than men.

They like the way that they can manipulate them, flatter them and ultimately use their sex against them.

In a way, they are as cynical as the Soviet state. All right, in London and New York wage slavery has glamorous trappings for some of those at the top – chilled Chardonnay in wine bars, sexy business suits, shiny cars.

They can shop in supermarkets instead of on the black market.

But, underneath all this glitter, it leads to the same grey dead-ends – a weakening of the marriage bond, dangerous scorn for the honourable profession of motherhood and, above all, the disastrous neglect of the next generation.

Dare to challenge this and you always get the same reply.

Just as Orwell's sheep in *Animal Farm* celebrated their own submission by bleating: "Four legs good – two legs better", working women will snarl: "You just want to chain us to the kitchen sink."

This stupid expression, like all slogans, is merely a substitute for thought.

Is there nothing in the home but a sink? What about nurturing children, teaching them the wisdom of centuries, not least showing young boys that women can be friends rather than simply servants or sex-objects?

In millions of homes, children are now being brought up by the television, by each other or – and this is the best case – by nannies.

This is a world where a mother can say (as one "working woman" did on BBC2 this week): "I'm not used to children. After all, I've only had them for five years."

More and more of the world's women are "not used to children" because they are too busy in offices and factories.

In the haunted, hooded eyes of the next generation – swift to turn to violence, foul-mouthed, scornful of gentleness, without grace or manners – we see the result.

8/3/96

Real sex education lesson

The sex war is over in America, according to the mighty *Washington Post*. In that case. it will probably be ending here too, quite soon.

Meantime, the *Post* has been counting the cost and the casualties.

In a vast national survey, it found that Americans regret the way that neither men nor women have much time for the real things of life, marriage and family.

Majorities of both sexes agreed it would be better if women could stay at home to take care of house and children.

Our Government, with its fanatical campaigns to send single mothers out to work, and its new scheme for tax funded corrals for all four-year-olds, seems determined to make its own mistakes rather than learn from those of others.

These policies are already discredited in the USA which gave birth to them.

3/3/98

Our rulers seem to hate everything that is normal and good nowadays. Handing divorce propaganda to tiny infants, as has happened in Durham, is only the latest sign of this.

Do you want your children to be homosexual? The State and the schools don't care about your feelings. Backed up by the broadcasters, they aggressively push the idea that sterile sodomy, leather bondage clubs and sex in public lavatories are just a normal lifestyle choice, much the same as deciding between a Ford or a Vauxhall. And they do this to young people without the experience or wisdom to know that it is a lie.

Later this year, in a so-called "free vote" for which we cannot punish them, MPs including alleged Conservatives will expose immature 16- and 17-year-olds to the tender mercies of predatory older homosexuals.

It's all part of a pattern. What was deviant behaviour 30 years ago is now being brought into the mainstream.

Do you want your daughters to go on the Pill when it's still illegal to have sex? The law says you can't stop them.

Do you want to apply loving discipline to your children, to enforce the moral code which you were brought up to believe in? Be careful. The authorities are quite capable of siding with your wayward youngster and setting him or her up on their own, free to take illegal drugs and indulge in under-age sex, at taxpayers' expense of course.

Do you think drug-taking is always wrong, because it is immoral and illegal? Then look at the propaganda being fed to the young with official permission, explaining how to take drugs "safely", and saying there is no real difference between legal alcohol and illegal Ecstasy.

Not only is this mad and misleading, it undermines the whole idea that drug-taking is a wrong act and tells the drug-taker he is the innocent victim of shadowy and evil pushers. And the Establishment's growing contempt for stable marriage and parenthood now reveals its latest, falsely smiling face, softening up the infants for the divorce or separation that our culture does *nothing* to discourage.

A new Charles Dickens is needed to portray the misery we are inflicting on ourselves, as cruel as Oliver Twist's workhouse, as the convict hulks in *Great Expectations*.

Then we might recognise the damage we are doing and stop being so smug about how civilised we are.

20/4/98

Why do we so seldom see the servants who look after Labour's aristocracy? Who is providing "quality childcare" for the Blair offspring while daddy runs the country and mummy sues daddy's Government?

Shouldn't there have been a nanny somewhere in last week's photo-opportunity when Gordon Brown borrowed a child's birthday to soften his steely image?

The child involved is the son of gazillionaire banker Gavyn Davies and political high-flyer Sue Nye. I am sure they are wonderful, responsible parents but their exciting lives cannot leave them as much time as they would wish with their three-year-old.

I think the reason the servants stay hidden is that this new superclass of socialist nobles cannot admit that they are exceptional.

They want to pretend that they are like all the other millions of couples, who each morning reluctantly lodge their tiny, protesting young with childminders or cheap nurseries. But they are not.

The new elite, Labour and Tory, have two careers because it is fun and fulfilling and it allows them to afford live-in nannies and big, gracious houses in fashionable areas with good state schools.

The millions do it because there is no other way they can afford their mortgages, their cars and the colossal taxes we are all compelled to pay for useless schools, heartless hospitals and helicopter-borne robocops.

I am convinced that great armies of women yearn to care full time for their own young but simply cannot afford to.

It hurts. It hurts so much that one woman in four has now decided that motherhood is impossible for her. She can't fit it into a life devoured by work, work, work.

So the most thoughtful and prudent people are just giving up on parenthood, leaving the job instead to state-subsidised lone mothers, many fighting a losing battle against a culture which urges their daughters to be sluts and their sons to be thugs.

Thus do we destroy our civilisation, without meaning to.

Yet it need not be like this. Britain is, or was, a uniquely happy nation largely because its elite realised they had a duty to help the less fortunate.

The time has now come for the new upper class to understand that their wealth and good fortune lay the same obligation upon them.

And, above all other things they must rush to the aid of the poor married family, scorned by fashion, undermined by easy divorce, stripped of its privileges by mistaken concessions to the unwed, unfairly taxed and riven by the now-compulsory need for a double income.

23/3/98

Which Labour politician's affair wrecked the marriage of a couple with young children quite recently? I wouldn't dream of telling you since it would only make things worse for all involved and open up old wounds.

Which homosexual minister prefers to keep his active sex life a secret? Don't ask me. As long as he doesn't choose to make propaganda out of his lifestyle, nor should anyone else. Which aide of the Prime Minister recently dumped his wife and children and fathered a child by a girlfriend? Which close colleague of Mr Blair has had several children out of wedlock and has no plans to marry? Again, that's their affair, in one case literally.

But the fact is that Mr Blair's circle contains rather a lot of people whose private family life is, or has recently been, highly unconventional.

I mention this because the Prime Minister claims that he likes the family and then wags his finger at the Press benches and says: "I challenge the media: don't use it as an excuse to dredge through the private lives of every public figure. Accept that whatever our individual weaknesses, our collective strength lies in making the institution of the family work for the good of Britain."

I don't remember the Labour Party urging the media to fall silent when it went through its long frenzy of exposing the private foibles of the Tory government on the flimsy excuse that John Major had called for a return to older standards. I shall certainly expect them to do so if it happens again.

But the truth is that the personal choices of Mr Blair's circle, so very unlike his own blameless home life, do have a bearing on his policy.

If your close friends and colleagues are divorced, cohabiting, homosexual or the parents of illegitimate children, it is very hard to stand up for traditional marriage while they are around.

It seems tactless and clumsy, pious and offensive to bring up the subject in their presence. Even if you only imply your approval for conventional morality, there will be uncomfortable moments.

It is far easier, far more "compassionate", to fudge the issue, to adopt fashionable views on morality even if you do not follow those views in your own personal life. And so marriage itself, the public declaration and bond without which men cannot be relied on to support and cherish wives and children, becomes something to be almost ashamed of, something which cannot be defended or strengthened.

And the numbers of one-parent families grow and grow, with consequences for the future that are worse than we can begin to imagine.

So, to all those in public life who have rejected the rules that the rest of us try to live by, a plea of my own. Please don't take it personally when the rest of us say we think you're wrong. We understand that life is complicated and difficult and we have our own weaknesses. But most people – especially children – simply cannot cope with a world without rules.

5/10/98

I am thinking of having a T-shirt made with Happy To Be A Homophobe stencilled across the front. I am sick and tired of the way our bigoted society discriminates against people like me and tries to force us to be ashamed of a perfectly reasonable point of view.

I long ago gave up trying to point out that the word "homophohia" is an ugly and dishonest invention, that it is insulting, misleading and hysterical.

Nobody would listen.

So, on the eve of the latest attempt to extend "gay rights", I decided to step right out of the closet and let the whole world know the truth. Which is this:

I am against the lowering of the homosexual age of consent to 16. If we are changing the age of consent we should be raising it upwards for everyone. It might help the young resist our culture's relentless pressure on them to climb into bed with each other or with older seducers.

I am against it because I do not think that the homosexual way of life is equal to heterosexual marriage.

I am against it for the same reason that I oppose the

promiscuous and sterile heterosexual way of life which has grown out of control since Roy Jenkins forced us to have a permissive society.

Why? Because marriage is a tough option, in which sexual pleasure is only part of the bargain, and to many people not the most important part.

Its main purpose is to produce, raise, nurture and educate the next generation. In return, society used to grant important privileges to the married. Those privileges, now whittled almost to nothing, were the foundation stones of our sexual morality.

This is not the place for a long and detailed argument about why I personally think that homosexual acts are wrong in themselves, though I would point out that the intricately designed and miraculous human body was obviously not intended for such a purpose.

But it is the place to say that it is a lie to suggest that I, or the millions who feel as I do, suffer from a personal loathing for individual homosexuals. It is a lie to suggest that our reasoned opinions, normal in civilised countries throughout the world, are in some way crazed or hysterical. A society in which homosexuality was normal would swiftly die out. I will not claim that "some of my best friends are homosexuals", though they may well be for all I know or care. I do not wish to know the details of their private sexual tastes, which are none of my business and which ought to be one of the least important things about them.

What I cannot accept is the attempt to mislead the young into the belief that the homosexual way of life is the equivalent of heterosexual marriage.

This is a dangerous untruth and those who spread it are doing something very wrong.
22/6/98

The two stupidest claims in Jack Straw's attack on the family, masquerading as support, are these: that the Government is not allowed to preach on moral matters and that ministers' private lives have anything to do with the issue.

The Government preaches *all the time* on moral topics. It is just that all its preaching is fiercely opposed to traditional morality, so it is called advice or guidance or health education or progressive thinking.

The Government preaches that it is a good thing for women to go out and become wageslaves, rather than bringing up their own children.

Its support for nurseries, its pressure on single mothers to get jobs, are central to this.

The government – together with the condom lobby, local authorities and most of the media – preaches that pills, abortions and french letters, rather than self-restraint, are the answer to under-age sex.

It acts as if the idea of chastity outside marriage is an outrageous and foolish concept, rather than a time-hallowed and highly sensitive response to the crude sexual appetites of irresponsible young men and thoughtless young women.

Any parents who try to defy this preaching find that the full weight of the law descends on their household, along with armies of social workers ready to allege sex abuse if they don't get their way.

Even once-sensible professions, such as the police and doctors, now refuse to support parents against their wayward young. Meanwhile, councils use public money to fund anti-marriage propaganda campaigns, alleging that huge numbers of marriages are defiled by domestic violence, on the basis of skewed and exaggerated statistics.

If a tenth of this effort were devoted to telling the young the old rules, then there would be no need for Mr Straw to recruit a new nanny army to go round instructing us on how to wipe our babies' bottoms, or to set up a helpline so that we can whinge down the telephone to a complete stranger about the problems of having a moody two-year-old.

What will these health visitors and helpline merchants be

telling us, by the way?

Are they for or against smacking? What about sarcasm? Are we allowed to smoke at home? How many units of alcohol are suitable while parenting? Can we make homophobic remarks in the presence of the children? Should we use environment-friendly cloth nappies or polluting disposable ones? Do we let our young watch *The Big Breakfast*?

Actually, it's none of their business. A free people should thumb its nose at such nonsense.

All we want is a government that stops undermining marriage and the family with destructive divorce laws and tax rules and that lets us alone to live a good, moral life according to principles which lasted 2,000 years until modern rulers decided to cast them aside.

And if they would do that, the whole Cabinet could spend its days and nights indulging in private sexual deviations, for all I care.

9/11/98

Three times a week, I think about emigrating to a country where some sanity still reigns. But where to go? A crazy new conformism has spread like ground elder, to the remotest ends of the earth.

A correspondent in New Zealand sends me a story from Auckland's main newspaper which begins: "Moves to get Auckland's sex industry off city streets have upset disabled people wanting equal access to its services."

Plans to banish the "industry" to basements and attics are under attack because "disabled people" argue that they are "as entitled as anyone to unimpeded access to sex industry premises".

Of course, political correctness is funny at first with its coy expressions and prim lack of humour. But when you examine it, you find a project designed to make certain thoughts unthinkable, unsayable and eventually unprintable. If you object to this, or dare to laugh at it, you are revealing yourself as an unacceptable, unkind, narrow person, whose views no longer need to be taken into account.

This is censorship of people rather than censorship of books, newspapers or broadcasting. As a result, it is both harder to attack and more powerful than any form of thought control since the dark ages.

12/4/99

Something is missing from the NSPCC's new campaign against child abuse. Research shows that all types of abuse are much more common in families where parents are unmarried.

When a woman has a series of "boyfriends" the danger is greatest of all.

According to a detailed study of case reports from the reputable legal journal *Family Court Reporter*, it is 33 times more dangerous for a child to be brought up by a woman and her "boyfriends" than by married parents. In cases where the abuse leads to the death of the child, the danger is even greater – 74 times higher where the mother had "boyfriends" rather than a husband.

Of course, married families are not immune from abuse but the logic of this suggests that marriage is the most effective protection a child can have.

Yet the NSPCC publicity does not distinguish between married families and others – suggesting that all homes are equally at risk. The NSPCC is a respected national institution and should put this right.

29/3/99

KOSOVO

Do men have to die and cities burn so that we can all watch the TV bulletins with an easy conscience? Are we really so foolish as to think that we have the power to drive evil from the world? Has NATO become the military wing of the Nine O'Clock News?

Rulers are not given their power to shed blood so that they can use it to make themselves feel good, or to seek to raise their poll ratings. They are given it so that they can protect their own citizens from peril and subjugation.

I do not, cannot care about Kosovo, not because I am a callous brute but because I do not have the power to enforce my moral code there – and nor does the NATO alliance. It is a full-time job to fight against the growing cruelty, licence, selfishness and violence which threaten to engulf our own small country.

To say that I cared about this Balkan snake-pit would be worthless posturing, designed to make me look compassionate in the eyes of the electronic mob who have surrendered their minds to the TV. I do not trust those who noisily beat their breasts about distant crises but neglect their own neighbours.

It doesn't even work. Since Bill Clinton and Tony Blair began their latest Nintendo war, life has grown much worse for the people it is supposed to help. With few to watch them the Serbs have increased their persecution of Albanians tenfold. Those who protest are sneeringly told: "Complain to NATO." It is a cruel but telling jibe and it makes my blood run cold because it cuts so close to the bone.

Science has yet to invent an evil-seeking missile, or a smart bomb that can select between bully and victim. Our hands–off, low-risk form of warfare is worse than useless in places such as the Balkans, where the bearers of terror are the pistol, the grenade, the scruffy, drunken "policeman" who hammers on the door before dawn, who torches your home and leads your menfolk away into the night and fog of official murder.

If you really want to fight such people, you must go there yourself. You must be that unfashionable thing, an imperialist. And you must stay for ever. For as soon as you leave, it will all start again.

We should know. With the approval of the Labour Party, we abandoned India to the greatest inter-communal massacres in history; abandoned Cyprus to inter-ethnic kidnapping and murder; abandoned Palestine to eternal conflict; abandoned Africa to Idi Amin, Kwame Nkrumah and the rest.

We are now abandoning the law-abiding people of Northern Ireland to the mafia rule of the IRA and UVF. Are we going to set up a protectorate of Kosovo, with no end to it?

The idea is ludicrous. So is the nonsense spouted by ministers that Slobodan Milosevic is another Hitler. Where are his great tank armies poised to invade Western Europe? Where are his squadrons of bombers ready to rain death on London, Liverpool and Belfast? Where are his battleships and fleets of submarines capable of strangling our food supplies? We went to war against Hitler not because he was a criminal murderer but because he threatened our liberty and independence. In the battle against him, we happily accepted the help of another criminal murderer, Josef Stalin. Beside Stalin's monstrous evil, Milosevic looks like a part-time amateur.

We know why the squalid draft-dodger Bill Clinton enjoys playing soldiers. It is to help his reputation at home, now blackened once again by credible allegations that he is a rapist.

But what moves our pacifist Prime Minister, who was a grown-up member of the Campaign for Nuclear Disarmament in the years when every British city was a target for Soviet H-bombs, and when Moscow's mighty Third Shock Army sat a few miles from our own small forces on the German plain?
29/3/99

Do the supporters of the mad Kosovo war really believe the things they say? I would love to put this to the test. When you've finished killing Milosevic with your mouth, would you care to join my International Brigade? Everyone is accepted, regardless of age, height, weight, flat feet, bad breath, sex or sexual "orientation".

Just leave all that you hold dear, as you are asking others to do, don a uniform, do a few weeks' basic training and get out there to prove you care. If you truly think that Milosevic is the new Hitler and that the events now unfolding in Kosovo are a re-run of the Holocaust, I don't think you have any choice. If we face another Third Reich what do your mortgage, your job, your next holiday or a whole skin matter?

My father's generation *had* to drop everything, to spend six years eating bully beef, shivering with cold and getting shot at, bombed and, quite often, killed or crippled, dealing with the real thing. My wife's uncle did not wait to be called up. He left safe neutral Switzerland and smuggled himself into Spain to risk his life for what he believed was the cause of justice and democracy – all honour to him, even though his own Republican side turned out to be pretty badly tainted in the end.

But all today's heroes need to do is damn Serbia in the pub and cheer the wide-screen TV as bombs fall on Belgrade. If they opened a recruiting office for a "Save Kosovo" brigade, I don't think anyone would turn up.

Then there's the question of the refugees now pouring out of Serbian territory. If you wanted this war you have quite a responsibility to these people. There's strong evidence that they were driven from their homes because of the ill-thought-out NATO action.

So, would you care to invite a Kosovar family into your home, indefinitely? More to the point, would Robin Cook, our warlike Foreign Secretary, like to welcome several Kosovar families into his spacious residence overlooking St James's Park? Will the Cabinet donate their taxpayer-provided flats and houses all over London?

Will the Prime Minister sacrifice his beloved Chequers and let some Kosovars use his nice new tennis courts to take their minds off the fact that they will never see their homes again? And Dorneywood and Chevening are ideal places to recover from being ethnically cleansed.

If Mr Blair and his colleagues think they have such a duty towards the Balkans, let them make a personal sacrifice to prove it. Otherwise, we might think it was all empty bluster by people who don't understand war, don't know history and who have got themselves into a stupid mess by trying to show off.

5/4/99

There's no such thing as a nice, kind war

Welcome to the world's first caring war, in which civilians die and soldiers don't, in which the weapons are smarter than the politicians, in which everything that goes wrong is either an accident or the other side's fault.

Wars are won by ruthless violence. Women and babies die in them. The only mercy is a swift victory. Wise people do not start wars and they fight them solely when their most vital interests are at stake and all else has failed.

But this was different. We broke our own rules and began bombing a sovereign state because we were so damned good and kind. Well, in that case, the butchery of innocents is something we simply cannot do. Where it happens we must own up swiftly, discipline those involved harshly and ensure that it does not happen again.

But do we? No, our chiefs dodge and fumble, make excuses, are slow to admit the truth and then confess quietly that it is bound to happen again.

This bloody folly lost all its moral justification when the first NATO bomb killed the first non-combatant. It now only continues because the pygmy leaders of the NATO democracies cannot think of a way out that will not make them look silly.

Well, too bad. They have bungled and, if they had any decency, they would admit it and seek an exit. If they do not, they will deserve everything they get.

The NATO alliance has now become a menace to itself. Its absurd spokesmen, who sound like the Apologies Department of a rather dim local authority, daily insult our intelligence.

If these events are "accidents" then they are, in that great cliche of our times, "accidents waiting to happen" and therefore not accidents at all. They were entirely predictable and I'll bet that the military predicted them in the private briefings they gave to our "leaders".

Yet each time they slay a civilian, they begin by saying that the Serbs did it. Then they mumble that, just maybe there could have been a mistake. Then they produce one of their ghastly snuff movies to show that a pilot flying at 10,000ft cannot see what he is bombing until it is too late.

Well, what a surprise. These pilots are rare men of courage and discipline who would give their lives if necessary, not because they believe in this bird–brained war but because they believe in doing their duty.

But their political masters, unfit for kingship, scared of the electronic mob which put them in power and which would drag them from office, would rather blow up a trainload of innocent foreigners, or strafe a convoy of refugees, than risk a single casualty among their own troops.

The idiotic statement that the few had to suffer to save the many is one of those which dies on the lips once you think about it – along the lines of "the operation was a success but the patient died" and that ghastly motto of the Vietnam war, "We had to destroy the village in order to save it".

The politicians want war without risks – to themselves. They want us to think they are decisive national leaders and world statesmen.

But they fear the effect on the focus groups and the opinion polls if they are seen to have sent their own citizens to their deaths.

19/4/99

Our state-monitored media have already started to pretend that a steadfast Tony Blair has won a great triumph in Kosovo. It is not true.

On the night of the peace deal, it was repeatedly stated that Serbia had got worse terms than it could have had before our 10-week campaign of terror against her civilian population.

But on several points, dealing with war crimes, elections in Kosovo and, above all, the make-up of the occupation force, the new plan is far vaguer than the old one.

When the skeleton of the agreement is fleshed out with detail, it may be even clearer that Mr Milosevec has actually gained by holding out.

The final result could well be a division of Kosovo between Russian and NATO forces, with Serbs in one area and Albanians in the other, which Mr Blair says is not acceptable. Well, we'll see. Does he, in fact, have a better plan? Does anyone? The supposedly civilised West has already caused quite enough harm in this dangerous region with its lofty schemes.

Crude mass shifts of population are foul and violent but we have helped to make them happen. They are the direct result of the idea that all the nations of Europe should decide their own futures within borders designed by diplomats. Ethnic cleansing, though carried out by brutes and murderers, is the outcome of Western good intentions.

Stupid American idealism, by destroying Europe's old empires and creating shoals of new statelets, turned the Continent into a seething pit of ethnic rivalry 80 years ago. Since then, a complex patchwork of races, religions, cultures and languages have been forced to tidy themselves up to suit their new frontiers.

But the tidying, which may look neat enough in an atlas,

means misery and tragedy for the people who get tidied.

It brought about the conditions in which Hitler flourished. It created angry and resentful minorities all over central and eastern Europe. It led to the nightmare exchange of population between Greece and Turkey in the Twenties and to the murderous mass expulsion of Germans from Poland and the Czech lands in 1945.

There has hardly been a decade this century without its quota of trudging refugees in Europe, trying to find a home on the right side of an ethnic boundary drawn up by well-meaning politicians. We and the Americans, behind the shield of the sea, have been among the few who have escaped – so far.

Has our pious war added to the sum of human happiness, or to the far greater sum of human misery? Consider this question, before awarding any prizes to any politician, particularly to Mr Blair, who has been so terribly brave about ordering American troops into battle.

7/6/99

Hurrah for the Russians. I never expected to hear myself saying this, since I have watched Moscow's soldiers at their worst; arrogant, murderous and hateful, spitting on freedom. Yet now I am grateful to their tiny Kosovo contingent for sticking a rusty bayonet into NATO's balloon of vanity and fake triumph. With a bold and witty gesture, they ruined a revolting vote-grabbing parade by the politicians of the West.

First, we watched the paunchy bureaucrat George Robertson, our Defence Secretary, scrambling heavily on to a tank to harangue the troops, who to their credit declined to applaud his pitiful attempts to sound like Winston Churchill. They are soldiers of the Queen, not soldiers of the Government, and Mr Robertson should have known it. And after him will no doubt come President Zipper and Princess Tony, and a gaggle of Euro-leaders, anxious for their photo opportunities next to the soldiers they did not dare to send into real battle.

The contemptible squabbling over whose troops would be first into Kosovo tells you all you need to know about the purpose of this war. Its aim has always been to polish up the images of President Zipper and Princess Tony at home. If you think it was about mercy and pity, then ask the poor, ethnically-cleansed Kurds of Turkey what NATO has ever done for them.

14/6/99

Now that our supposed friends, the Kosovo Albanians, are beating Serb grannies to death, harassing harmless elderly professors and have ethnically cleansed all but a few Serbs from their ancestral homes, isn't it time all those who supported our pro-Albanian war began to wonder whether our action was justified?

Two months ago I invited my critics – who insisted "something must be done" – to re-examine their views once eight weeks had gone by. I believe the evidence clearly shows that we have replaced one brutal injustice with another, at a terrible price.

We cast aside international law by bombing a sovereign country and have bogged down a huge part of our dwindling army in a place where they ought never to have been sent – and may not now leave for years.

23/8/99

96

HISTORY

Why I am a man for all seasons

How I scorn the foolish bias of forecasters in favour of hot sunny days. Perpetual sunshine is all very well for movie stars and invalids, but I like weather.

This is an extraordinarily beautiful time of year. The countryside takes on a tawny, exciting look. The bones of the hills are visible through the leafless trees. Stars and the moon are ten times brighter and the late sunrises are packed with melodrama.

Familiar landscapes, edged with fog, become eerily different. Cities look older and grander in the sombre daylight and shop windows glow more brightly.

The short days emphasise the warm light of civilisation and home. There is no better season to go to football matches; the surrounding sky growing black against the floodlights during the second half; the walk home in the crisp, chilly dark. It is the best season to take a long train ride, especially into the mysterious lands of Central Europe.

In these places and even in remote parts of our own country I sometimes have a compelling sensation that ordinary time has somehow fallen into step with eternity.

This happened to me most powerfully in the astonishing winter of 1989. It was not actually Christmas when I stood on a snowy field in Prague and watched the peaceful return of liberty and truth to that dark, haunted city but it felt as if the angels were a good deal closer to Earth than usual.

It was the same on the morning that I set off for Bucharest, a few weeks later. I was frightened half out of my wits, but the long winter's journey across Romania, past shepherds in prehistoric fleece cloaks, towards the sound of big guns made me think of T. S. Eliot's austere words:

> "A cold coming we had
> of it, just the worst time
> of the year for a journey,
> and such a long journey,
> the ways deep and the
> weather sharp, the very
> dead of winter."

But a journey with hope at the end of it.
9/12/96

Never forget to mention the war

The most heartbreaking letters I receive are from those who served in the war, or lost loved ones in the conflict, which end with the soft, despairing words "I wonder why we bothered".

One such letter recently came with a copy of the harsh unbearable death notification which relatives used to receive from the Army Council. Those who had to open such a message, on a cold, grey, rationed morning must have wondered how they could go on living. As Tennyson wrote: "Ghastly in the drizzling rain, on the bald street, breaks the blank day."

If anything fortified them it was the knowledge that their bereavement was justified by the good, perhaps even noble cause for which we fought. And so they went off to their hard tasks.

Now we have a Foreign Secretary who announces that he doesn't mention the war. Well, to hell with him. I spent last week in Germany, a country I love for its beauty, its architecture, its music and its many contributions to civilisation. It is also heartening and pleasant to see how democracy, law and freedom have taken root there. But during that journey I paused at several places – at the Buchenwald concentration camp which lies three miles from Weimar, this year's "European City of Culture"; at a spot in Munich where passers-by used to be compelled to give the Nazi salute or be thrown into prison; at the gloomy but solid ruins of the Nuremberg stadium where Hitler raved against the Jews; at the place of shame in Berlin where students (who else?) gathered in 1933 to burn books they were too bigoted to read.

Then I thought of the square miles of graves, of the ruined lives, of the loss and the courage, and I thanked every one of those people who fought and lost all, so that I could write this and say this and think this, and I would think it a foul shame not to mention the war. And you can count on me to do so, regularly, even if Robin Cook doesn't like it.

22/2/99

MONARCHY

Princess should keep out of this moral minefield

Hush, hush, whisper who dares, Princess Diana is saying she cares – again. This time she is caring her heart out in Angola, a country she can hardly have heard of much before last Wednesday and which has not heard of her – trying to get landmines banned.

Who can possibly object? Angola is full of grotesquely maimed people, many of them women and children whose limbs have been torn off by these merciless weapons. The hardest heart must be moved to pity by the sight of this cruelty.

Yet there are powerful arguments against her stance, which the civilised world must understand. The pity is that Diana's involvement has driven reason and knowledge away – as the rash minister who dared criticise her has discovered.

Attacking Diana is like assailing Nelson Mandela and Mother Teresa simultaneously while lighting up in a non-smoking restaurant. Her many supporters are so bewitched that they cannot see that Diana is a rather ordinary woman deeply in love with herself. They automatically turn in wrath on anyone who dares criticise her holy name.

Even so, it is necessary to attack her. For her Queen of Hearts image is built upon a dreadful, phoney idea and is calculated to turn good-hearted citizens into dupes. The idea is that "caring" as noisily as possible about other people's misfortunes is itself a virtue, equal to secret charity, unsung courage and self-sacrifice. It leads rapidly to the notion that the more you care, the better you are and that your moral worth can be judged by the strength of your opinions.

And this lends itself to the obvious, simple solution to every problem facing the world. There are millions in poverty, so raise taxes to give them more money. People are knifed and shot in the streets, so ban knives and guns. Nuclear weapons are hideous, so let us scrap ours. And now this: landmines, planted in places such as Angola by callous warlords, are maiming the innocent. So ban them, too.

But to care is not just to weep especially in front of cameras and microphones. To be genuinely concerned about the world's problems, you must understand them and recognise that the obvious, emotional reaction may not quite have the effect intended.

There is no real difference between the Greenham Common Women's half-witted campaign against the defences of democracy and Diana's espousal of the Red Cross campaign against mines – except that the Greenham Common women were aggressively unattractive, while Diana is the opposite, and tinged with royalty, too.

Because it is all about second-hand, cheap, show-off morality the gospel of caring – which now unites Greenham Common and Kensington Palace – ignores the existence of evil.

It cannot understand that the ideas in people's minds are more important than the weapons in their hands. It cannot grasp that an H-bomb in the arsenal of the USSR is far worse than one in the armouries of the USA, Britain or France. It fails to see that banning guns and knives will not halt the forward march of selfish brutality on our streets.

It cannot grasp that a world-wide ban on landmines will be observed only by lawful countries, while the rest continue to make, sell and lay them by the million. Nazi Germany, the USSR, Communist China, Iraq, North Korea and many others have taken the view that treaties should be obeyed only when it suits them. Other such regimes are bound to arise.

Angola is a ghastly museum to post-colonial chaos, failed Marxism, tribal hatred and cynical Cold War rivalry. The mines which poison its landscape are a symptom of human wickedness, which will never come to an end and which will certainly not be abolished because a pretty princess has patted the cheek of a maimed and beautiful little girl.

16/1/97

Queen weeps for all our yesterdays

Various oafs and levellers sneer at the Queen and her family for crying as the royal yacht *Britannia* was needlessly and stupidly paid off for ever.

The innuendo here, which some have been crude enough to make openly, is that the Queen can cry over a lump of metal while she did not do so over the death of the blessed Saint Diana of the minefields.

Well, Her Majesty was not being filmed when she received the news of Diana's death, nor during the Princess's funeral service. These were, rightly, private moments. But that is not all. If she is anything like most British people (and I am pretty sure that she is), she was not mourning the end of a collection of plates, rivets and planks.

Her heart was touched by that sense of utter loss – wrongly dismissed as nostalgia – which now affects so many of us.

Familiar and kindly things depart. There is never anything we can do about it. The planners and the modernisers have made sure of that.

The motorway is driven through the lovely wood and the ancient trees crash to the ground. The honoured regiment is disbanded. The church is invaded with guitars and amplifiers. The friendly corner shop is forced out of business by hypermarkets and mad regulations. We gather round our last rib roast and try to laugh.

As each dismal bureaucratic day passes, we become exiles in our own country. That is why the Queen wept, and why millions of others, watching the miserable moment on TV, were damp-eyed in sad solidarity with her.

15/12/97

Sneaky road to a republic

Watch out for what seems to be turning into a regular Government technique for damaging the monarchy.

STAGE ONE: Put the throne in a difficult or embarrassing position. Try identifying Labour with the "People's Princess", or use the Queen to announce a dangerous change in foreign policy over Kashmir, which hurts our relations with India while winning some votes in marginal constituencies.

STAGE TWO: Watch the fun for a few days, as the Queen is subjected to nasty public attacks, hostile opinion polls and the usual chorus of snide commentators suggesting that she is out of touch and fuddy duddy and really ought to be thinking about retirement.

STAGE THREE: Having lowered Her Majesty into a tub of slime and left her there to struggle, slowly winch her out and leak stories about how concerned you are and how your skilled spin doctors are coming to the aid of Buckingham Palace, which of course cannot cope on its own. Then take advantage of the monarchy's decency, fairness and restraint which prevents the Queen or her aides from complaining about the shabby treatment you have inflicted on them.

If the Prime Minister and his pals do this often enough over the next few years the dignity and authority of the crown will grow fainter and more threadbare.

And, by the time Tony is finally ready to leave Downing Street, guess who will be ready to take the job of first People's President?

20/10/97

Downing Street declares that it now looks down on the "tacky exploitation" of the dead Princess Diana. This is obviously a different Downing Street from the one which cooked up the tacky phrase "People's Princess" and wrung every last drop of political advantage from the Princess's death and funeral.
26/2/98

Now we are told that the Queen, who sensibly didn't even know the time of the England–Argentine game when she was unfairly quizzed by a reporter, sat in her Edinburgh palace heckling the TV on the night of the match.

Did Downing Street get Her Majesty on her pager and tell her she was dead meat if she didn't wise up to the People's Sport?

If so, they have blundered yet again. For she was being Queen of Scotland at the time and it is well known that her Scottish subjects would support Botswana if they were beating England.
6/7/98

The poor, poor Queen. On Friday, she had a close encounter with a McDonald's burger bar, though she luckily avoided having to bite into one of these warm, slippery sandwiches while clutching it with a gloved hand. Next month, she will be spotted at a suburban Co-Op buying a lottery ticket. Soon afterwards, she will be waving a pugil-stick about on *Gladiators* (the Blairs' favourite viewing).

Meanwhile, guess who will be trying out the suites aboard the Royal Train and demanding a bigger plane than the Queen, so that he can get his ego aboard?
3/8/98

Don't bow to this dictatorship of grief

This could be our last chance to overthrow the weird dictatorship of grief which began on the day Princess Diana was driven into a concrete pillar by a drunken man.

If we do not resist and reject the attempt to canonise and sanctify her – and soon – we shall be stuck with it for at least a generation.

All kinds of folk, from politicians to businessmen, from militant lesbians to astrologers and quack doctors, will use her to manipulate us or fleece us.

It is not yet fitting or proper to criticise this poor unhappy woman, that time will come, much later, when we can decide what sort of person Diana was.

But it is not only proper but vital to be clear, right now, about what Diana Spencer was not.

She was not a saint. Highly publicised charity work does not confer holiness however much the camera loves you.

And real saints do not attract the sort of bitter, spiteful people who write me unpleasant, spittle-flecked letters if I breathe a word of criticism of their heroine.

She was not a political figure. Like most people, she knew little of the world and never understood the important frontier between private kindness and wise public policy.

Her understandable compassion for the victims of landmines and Aids does not automatically mean that all landmines are bad or that all victims should be treated as martyrs.

She was not a victim. Having been brought up in the small, cynical, divorce-prone, dynasty-obsessed world that is all that remains of a once-great aristocracy, she cannot have had many illusions about the pitfalls of a royal marriage.

Her memory belongs not to the nation or the "people" but to her immediate family. Let them mark the sad anniversaries of her birth and death in dignity and in private.

If anyone else feels they must commemorate the occasion,

then let them do a good deed in secret. We have no need of memorial gardens, coins or anything of that sort and we should not be afraid to say so.

26/6/98

Congratulations to the Queen Mother on her overdraft, said to be £4 million. I rejoice that she continues to live as royalty should, enjoying the good things in life on behalf of us all. I hope her daughter shows a similar defiance to the creepy modernisers who are now trying to turn her into a part of the Labour Party machine.

I am sure the Queen Mother needs no help from me in keeping a clear conscience. This sum would be small repayment for the part she and her husband played in keeping this country united and free through years of peril and uncertainty.

22/3/99

For once, a cupboard with no skeletons

When TV profiles a famous figure of the past, you can be sure it wants to pull him down. War heroes, great statesmen, diplomats and distinguished authors – all of them have been given the treatment.

They each turn out to have been secret perverts, secret Nazis, secret wife-beaters, horrid to their children and ungrateful to their friends and colleagues.

This isn't terribly difficult to do. A TV biography of Jesus Christ himself could no doubt dig up the occasional damaging incident and focus upon it. An interview with Judas Iscariot would certainly throw a new light on Our Lord, and some of the guests at the wedding in Cana might have a thing or two to say about His brusque treatment of His mother.

So you could sympathise with the makers of last week's moving and surprising profile of King George VI. Try as they might, they could come up with nothing to level against him except that he was sometimes bad-tempered and had a stammer. They also dragged up an old baseless claim that his father, George V, deliberately made his sons' life a misery.

George VI was exactly what he seemed to be: a modest, straightforward, kindly, utterly decent gentleman, who had the great sense to woo and win the perfect wife, the steely and indomitable woman who has survived him for almost half a century and — I'll bet — misses him every day of her life. He was also a good father who sought solace from family life in the midst of turmoil.

He never wanted to be King, especially when the task was thrust upon him by his worthless, charming brother. Yet he was the best monarch of modern times, who richly deserved Winston Churchill's funeral wreath bearing nothing but the terse and tremendous words "For valour".

In the end the job killed him, which is why I am still angered by the persecution of the Queen Mother about her overdraft, and about a number of sour resentful letters I have received from readers who disagree with my defence of that overdraft.

To them, I point out the following: she sacrificed her husband and decades of lost companionship to the national good — and don't you forget it. Her financial affairs are her own business. The taxpayer has always benefited hugely from the deal under which the vast income of the Crown estates goes to the State in return for the civil list.

And if the Queen Mother hadn't spent the money wisely on champagne and horses, the state would only have squandered it on schools which can't even teach children to read, or some other dreary futility.

17/5/99

Playboys cannot be Kings

Holidays say so much about us. And Prince Charles's raffish Mediterranean jaunt has quite put me off him.

I do try to be loyal to the poor, tortured heir to the throne. I have braved the venom of the Diana maniacs to suggest that she had her faults. I have admired his stands for proper buildings, traditional prayer and the countryside.

But, oh dear, this is all a bit much. I know our mean and nasty Government have turned the lovely Royal Yacht into a crummy museum but that doesn't mean Charles has to summer aboard a Greek millionaire's gin palace.

Nor does it mean he has to do so with his mistress in what looks suspiciously like an attempt to soften us up for a future Queen Camilla. If marriage doesn't matter any more, then nor does monarchy. A discreet affair might just have been bearable but this is the road to abdication and a republic.

And then there is the problem of his entourage. This is a wonderful collection, largely drawn from what I call the Couldn't Care Less Classes, including a weedy young hooray who admits to snuffling cocaine.

These people are not ideal company for a future King, let alone for two future Kings.

Nor should young William prance around like a playboy in wraparound shades, which make him look as if he were heir to the throne of Ruritania or Monaco, not to a proper crown.

The sensible monarchs of this century have not been members of the braying aristocracy: George V and George VI, Elizabeth II and her mother, have all been very middle class. They have been surrounded by teak-faced, lean old courtiers whose stuffiness looks rather comforting when you set them beside the unstuffy Tom Parker Bowles.

Even their palaces, castles and country houses had a suburban feel. They holidayed in their own country as often as not. They did their time in the Armed Forces. They didn't go to Eton, probably because their advisers realised that this would identify them too closely with one narrow section of society.

Now they are starting to look and behave like mere wealthy playboys, brats on yachts. There is no better fuel for the engines of class hatred and spiteful republicanism.

Is there nobody who can warn them in time?

13/9/99

EDUCATION

Imagine yourself coming round in a hospital casualty department, your memory a blank, your pockets empty or your handbag gone. Perhaps you can still read and count, perhaps not. In this world of scattered families and long-distance travel, how will you ever find out who you are? And what use will you ever be again, to yourself or anyone else?

More and more, Britain is like just such a patient, a country lost in amnesia, a people who have suffered a collective blow on the head which has wiped out our understanding of who we are and what we are for.

Unless we swiftly find a cure, then we will be adrift in a world only too ready to take advantage of our weakness.

The strange thing about this is that we have submitted so willingly to this mental castration that some of our own people have keenly sought to blot out the real past, and reshape our history into a grey mush of social reform and gender studies.

When communism tried to steal the history of Poland the furious parents risked their liberty to set up "flying universities" where the truth about the nation's history was taught in secret.

Yet our great free universities, our publishing houses and, above all, our schools participate with fierce joy in the extirpation of the true history of this country.

The latest episode in this chapter of national shame is the dropping of the British Political History syllabus by examination boards.

Before that, many of the most momentous episodes in the history of this country were quietly squeezed from the curriculum by the clever trick of making them optional. How many teachers, how many schools, how many pupils are going to opt for the longer course, the tougher exam, the more detailed reading?

Those who do seek the truth will find literature which offers a carefully doctored version of the past. The *Oxford Children's Encyclopaedia*, for example, constantly soft-pedals the giant civilising achievements of Britain and its empire, while offering sympathetic and apologetic biographies of communist leaders.

A mainstream history textbook offered to British secondary schools reprints a communist anti-war propaganda painting about the horrors of the Blitz, representing the opinion of a microscopic defeatist minority at the time.

A schools video produced last year on the Forties barely gives a walk-on part to Winston Churchill, a man who is being steadily written out of modern history because he does not fit the fashionable myth that the Tories sympathised with the Nazis and the Left were the only people who opposed Hitler.

This myth, very different from the truth, has been one of the great engines behind the constant bombardment of ill-advised "reform" imposed on everything from our currency to our penal system.

Labour's role in the rise of Hitler was consistently to vote against the rearmament measures which narrowly saved this country from slavery in 1940.

Stalin's insane orders to the German Communist Party, to refuse to co-operate with the Social Democrats, virtually ensured the Nazis would come to power in 1933.

This would be mirrored, six years later, in the joint victory parade staged by Nazi and Red Army troops in the then-Polish city of Brest, and the efficient supply of Soviet oil to Germany which fuelled the Nazi Blitzkrieg and the bombers which tore the heart out of London.

But millions of supposedly educated people know nothing of this, and are unaware that the one country which behaved with honour and courage when the fate of the world was being decided was Britain.

And the reason for this lies in a long history of independence and defiance, in which we repeatedly overcame the most astonishing odds to survive and triumph.

If the British people of 1940 had known nothing of Drake and Marlborough and Nelson, of Queen Elizabeth I and William Pitt, of Waterloo, whose anniversary is today, would they have imagined for a moment that they could stand alone against the Third Reich?

And Churchill's great speeches, decisive in crushing all suggestions of a peace treaty during the pivotal summer of 1940, were founded on his wide and deep knowledge of that past.

Just as important, they were couched in a high-octane language which would have been beyond anyone who had not been schooled in Shakespeare, the King James Bible, Milton, Wordsworth and Tennyson – now almost as unfashionable as proper history.

The great socialist historian A.J.P. Taylor, in his history of the period, tried to sum up Winston Churchill in a footnote. Without intending to, and against his Left-wing instincts, he found himself writing the words: "The saviour of his country." Taylor knew in his bones that this was the truth. Could another Churchill – worth 30 squadrons of Spitfires – grow up in the Britain of today? Would he know the facts, let alone the mighty rhythms of the English language, necessary to keep us off our knees? Would anyone understand what he was talking about?

Just try if you can to imagine the ghastly world of perverted science and racial extermination which would have resulted from a British surrender in 1940. As the American poet Alice Duer Miller said at the time: "I am American bred. I have seen much to hate here – much to forgive. But in a world where England is finished and dead, I do not wish to live."

Those who have made a modern Churchill impossible knew what they were doing. Their continental ideas – state control, regimentation, bureaucracy, government interference in the smallest parts of life – were blocked in the past by what they called "prejudice" – the determined opposition of the voters.

This is one of their favourite words, designed to suggest that people who hold common-sense opinions are bone-headed oafs, mental cavemen who resist change out of tribal instinct or plain stupidity.

But what they deride as "prejudice" is often nothing of the kind. On the contrary, it is the piled-up wisdom of the centuries, the fruit of the rich store of experience we call history. It is our owner's manual, our map, our index and our dictionary. Without it, we can barely lace our shoes.

Amnesiacs, of course, have no prejudice. But they have nothing else, either – except the ideal qualifications to serve as the slaves of others.

18/6/96

Size doesn't matter

Yet again we have a huge fuss about class sizes in schools. And yet again I must point out that the only serious research shows that it makes very little difference. What is important is the method of teaching.

The current fashion in state primary schools, sitting children round tables to waste time, while teacher goes slowly from group to group, is a failure. If we got rid of it, results would improve instantly. But teachers seem to think it beneath their dignity or perhaps "elitist" to stand by a blackboard and teach the whole class.

By the way, the Government's pledge to cut class sizes will come true in the end anyway because the birth rate is falling.

25/5/98

What is a promise from Tony Blair worth? The story which follows may help you to answer this question. I make no comment upon it.

In late 1996, Harriet Tillson wrote to Mr Blair, then Leader of the Opposition. She was worried about her daughters, who are being educated at private schools under the Assisted Places Scheme. She could not possibly afford to pay for this herself.

For her, as it was for many thousands or others, the scheme was a godsend. It gave her children the equality of opportunity Labour is so keen on and ensured that their talents were not wasted or lost in a substandard local authority school.

As a Labour supporter and voter, she wanted to be sure that her party's plan to abolish the scheme would not hurt her daughters.

Harriet received a reassuring reply from Mr Blair's office. I have it in front of me now and Downing Street confirms that it is authentic.

"We do not wish to disrupt the education of individual pupils," it says. "Any children already on the scheme will continue to receive support until the end of their education."

Like many others, Harriet's children attend a school which takes pupils from 7 to 18. She was reassured by the letter, and duly voted Labour on May 1.

When she found that her younger child will in fact lose her place at 11, rather than being allowed to continue till 18. Harriet got in touch with her MP, Ben Bradshaw (Lab, Exeter).

Here is a quotation from Mr Bradshaw's letter to Education Secretary David Blunkett, which he copied to Mr Blair. Note that this is a Labour MP, not me, saying this: "I am in a very difficult position because my constituent was assured by the Prime Minister when he wrote to her... to assure her that any children on the scheme will continue to receive support until the end of their education.

"However, as you know we are only guaranteeing places until the age at which children would normally change schools – either 11 or 13. This is clearly not the same as the original promise given to my constituent. She, understandably, feels that she was misled before the election on this policy."

Harriet has now left the Labour Party. She did not seek to publicise her case, which I found out about by accident.

23/2/98

A comprehensive guilt

For years, I have been saying that Labour's education policy was bad for the poor. Before the election, my colleague Stephen Pollard wrote an excellent pamphlet making the same point – that the comprehensive system favours the wealthy.

Why is this? Because the rich can buy their children a good education in three ways. They can pay fees, they can buy a house in the catchment area of a good comprehensive, or they can pretend to support state education while quietly spending a fortune on private tutors.

Now, the Labour-friendly journalist Mary Ann Sieghart has discovered that the state system may not be good enough for her own children. She quotes, but does not name, a Labour MP plunged in gloom because it is politically difficult for him to go private. She has also outed a number of "right-on London professionals" who have "sacrificed their ideology for their children's futures" – socialist speak for buying better schooling than the state provides.

She says these include Jon Snow, the presenter of Channel Four News, favourite TV bulletin of the politically correct, plus a whole crowd of unnamed "barristers, bankers, media folk and political advisers".

My heart fails to bleed for this lot, especially because they can afford to deal with the problem. And though I welcome Ms Sieghart's conversion, I would like to make this point.

If you are rich and socialist you shouldn't feel guilty about sending your children to private schools. You should feel guilty about supporting a government that deliberately, systematically and brutally makes it impossible for the children of the poor to get a good education.

You should be guilty about the mad destruction of hundreds of good grammar schools, and the monstrous abolition of the Assisted Places Scheme.

30/11/98

A degree of stupidity we don't need

What is wrong with elitism? Grown-up countries need elites who cannot be fooled by spin doctors and advertising men. They need people who can stand against the tide of fashion and say, without fear, that the emperor is striding down the street in the nude.

Universities, which taught people to answer the vital question "Is it any good?", were a great defence against mob rule. This, I suppose, is why they were so high on the target lists of Britain's cultural revolution.

Not only are they under heavy political pressure to discriminate against pupils from independent schools, where some sort of standards still exist, they are reduced to offering courses on surfing or allowing students to get MA degrees by watching old episodes of *The Sweeney*.

I cannot really blame Alan Jepson, the man who plans to write 20,000 words on this festival of yelling and flared trousers. He is only doing what the Government seems to want him to do. But in years to come, when real knowledge and understanding have died and we are lost in a moronic inferno of drivel and cruel laughter, those responsible for destroying the universities will bear a heavy burden of blame.

12/4/99

Estate agents will tell you that a good school will hugely increase house prices in its catchment area. This sort of selection, by wealth, is perfectly acceptable to Princess Tony.

But what we can't have is selection by ability. That doughty enemy of good schooling, David Blunkett, has seen to that. Under regulations drafted by him, good schools can be – and are being – banned from choosing pupils on merit rather than the size of their parents' borrowing power. Ugh.

9/8/99

A-level gold is losing its lustre

How long before sixth formers are getting so many A-levels, at such high grades, that they have to carry them away in wheelbarrows like inflated German marks in the Twenties? I am afraid there can be no serious doubt that A-level exams are not as tough as they used to be. Schools can say what they like but employers and universities both report that youngsters with good grades do not live up to them.

How can you get a geography A-level if you do not know what east and west are? How can someone with a grade A in maths fail a first-year course in the same subject once he gets to college? These things are happening. As for employers, Ruth Lea of the Institute of Directors tells me that they are deeply concerned at the failings of teenagers who come to them with high marks.

This is not an attack on the young people who have most certainly worked their hearts out for these exams and then spent a summer of horrible suspense awaiting the results. It is not their fault. They have been betrayed.

It is hurtful to point out the dismal truth. But it would be a far greater offence to them and to future generations to stay silent about this. If our nation sinks into poverty and decline in the years to come because our rivals still have good education and we do not, our grandchildren will not thank us for pretending that all was well.

The interesting question is why so many people want this subject ignored or want to deny the obvious. If weather forecasters daily predicted golden sunshine and warm breezes and the reality was freezing winds and slanting sleet, we should pretty soon want to know what they were playing at. If inflation figures claimed that we had a stable currency and the price of a trolley-load of groceries doubled in a year, we should demand an inquiry. If official figures showed that Virgin Trains kept perfect time and that the motorways were free of cones, we would howl with mockery.

But in this far more crucial national index we are told to ignore the evidence of our own wits. There are many reasons why – but part of the explanation is that some people genuinely don't realise what is happening.

More than 30 years after most primary schools abandoned traditional learning, we now have many teachers and parents, and even university lecturers, who do not know that their spelling is poor, their arithmetic pitiful and their grammar atrocious. Who is there to tell them?

23/8/99

LIBERTY

Howard's way is a violent assault on our liberty

Terrible and stupid things have been done in this country in the name of civil liberties – for example, the undermining of proper responsible juries, the legal obstruction of reasonable police inquiries, the exposure of witnesses to intimidation and the abolition of the death penalty for remorseless murderers.

Because of this, many of us are ready to stop our ears to the reflex whining of the mainly Left-wing and modish liberty lobby. Far too many of these people were only too happy to apologise for repression, provided it was done in the name of socialism.

Some of us, in fact, might be tempted to support Home Secretary Michael Howard's new Police Bill simply because playwright Harold Pinter does not like it.

We would be terribly mistaken to do so. Even Mr Pinter, like a stopped clock, is sometimes accidentally right. This Bill, wafted through Parliament so far by an unhealthy and unthinking "tough on crime" consensus of Labour and Tory, is a repellent and sneaky thing, which should be chased back into the dark corner whence it came.

If it is passed, policemen will be able to bug and enter property – yours or mine – on the say-so of a Chief Constable. In other words, they will be able to *authorise themselves* to do so. No other country with the rule of law gives its police this sort of right. Our European neighbours, who almost all have recent practical experience of police states, do not. Nor do the USA, Canada, Australia or New Zealand, whose freedoms are founded on the ancient liberties of England.

Quite rightly, they require independent authorisation by an

outsider, almost always a judge, for such operations. This is a sensible British tradition, designed to stop the concentration of too much power in too few hands.

It is one of the foundation stones of liberty that the guardians of the State must themselves be restrained by a higher power.

The founders of the USA enshrined all this in their Constitution and Bill of Rights because, in a new nation, they felt they should take nothing for granted. As a result, the US Supreme Court would simply throw out this nasty Bill after no more than a brief glance.

But Britain's unwritten constitution does take things for granted. It assumes that we are free to act as we wish unless the law specifically says we are not.

It assumes that the powers of the Crown and the Government are always beneath the rule of law.

A thousand years of tradition and custom, reinforced by the glory of the common law, defend us while we sleep. This is a fine and rather moving thing, and we are rightly proud of it.

But it has always been built upon the vigilance of the stiff-necked and troublesome British people. And lately it has not been quite so easy to rely on this as it once was.

Softened by affluence, so accustomed to freedom and safety that we think they are a fact of nature, like the earth and the air, we have grown slack about defending ourselves.

At the same time. the cause of freedom has fallen into the hands of the Left, who like to wave the banner of liberty while planning to undermine it.

So only a few convincing voices have so far been raised in protest. The most notable and courageous of these has been Lord Browne-Wilkinson, a Law Lord, who says of himself: "I am tough on crime. But I am steely on freedom." This is what he told his fellow peers in November: "The state, its officers, the police – anybody – have no greater power to enter property than has any other person.

"Officers of the Crown cannot invade our property. If they

do, the courts regard it as illegal. That is the only safeguard against State intervention in our privacy. In this Bill, that safeguard is being eroded very substantially.

"The common law will be able to do nothing if the right to invade our property is conferred on the State, in the form of the police, with no prior approval from an independent party."

How can anyone argue against this? Judges are not likely to refuse the necessary warrants if the police make out a good case. But their independence gives them the power and the right to stop or delay the action if they believe it is going too far.

Mr Howard, supported by his shadow, Jack Straw, has claimed that the Bill merely formalises guidelines already in existence.

This is partly correct, and quite shocking in itself. These guidelines, issued in 1984, have already been used to permit as many as 2,000 bugging operations a year by police and Customs.

But the truth is that the guidelines are far more narrowly-drawn than the new Bill, and the new law could, for instance, be used against groups of bypass protesters, just as easily as it could be used against drug traffickers.

Once all this would have been less disturbing. Our police forces were made up mainly of plain, moral human beings recruited from a liberty-loving people who knew their own history and shared a broadly conservative view of life. Not now. Years of reorganisation and graduate intake have transformed them into a morally-neutral body, full of politically correct but rather ignorant senior officers, many of whom view themselves as separate from, and above, the public they are supposed to serve.

They parade about in military uniforms, festooned with billy-clubs and handcuffs, to emphasise their separateness. Left to themselves can they really be trusted to handle our freedoms with care?

It is not especially surprising that Labour MPs, themselves now cowed by a semi-dictatorial regime of obedience and silence, have failed to protest against this assault on liberty. Socialism and freedom have always been uneasy bedfellows.

The real shock is the silence of the Tories in the Commons, who have yet to raise their voices, and have very little time left to do so.

15/1/97

Is liberty safe in Labour hands?

There is now a threat to the liberty of the citizen in this country. This is a serious charge to make and I have thought very hard before doing so. Several events during the past week have convinced me this Government is indifferent or even hostile to our traditional freedoms. And since so much of our democracy depends on convention and restraint rather than law, this is cause for alarm.

The most disturbing was the apparently organised howling down of a Tory MP in Parliament. The Deputy Speaker had to call for order 23 times in 30 minutes. Witnesses say this does not give a full picture. The MP, Oliver Letwin, wanted to raise the behaviour of Robin Cook towards his secretary.

A mysteriously large number of Labour MPs, including several of the "Stepford Wives" type so rightly criticised by Brian Sedgemore last week, barracked and interrupted so that Mr Letwin could not be heard in the chamber.

No democrat should behave thus. It was a favourite tactic of communists during their takeovers of Poland, Czechoslovakia and East Germany. It is disgusting and alien and I am still waiting for Mr Blair to disavow it.

Set this beside the Lord Chancellor's heavy-footed call for censorship, also yet to be condemned on the record. Note also the criticism of the Opposition for being "trivial" by the

Premier's friend Peter Mandelson. The Opposition has the perfect right to choose its own methods. It is simply none of Mr Mandelson's business.

And do not forget the needless plan to incorporate the European Human Rights Charter into British law, which actually threatens to reduce our liberties: the furtive legalisation of a Euro-police force with huge powers; the new driving licence which is obviously an embryo identity card; and the plans to snuff out the independent element in the Lords.

Almost as sinister is the bullying of the Commons by holding referendums on Bills nobody has seen and the increasing introduction of party-controlled list systems for the election of the new toy parliaments of this disunited Kingdom.

Mr Blair's circle seized hold of Labour by crushing opposition and restricting free speech. They seem to think they can become the permanent Government of Britain by the same methods. Let us hope they are wrong.

9/2/98

Too much democracy can destroy freedom. Nobody should ever forget that Adolf Hitler came to power by purely democratic means and persuaded the German parliament to cut its own throat.

This is why Tony Blair's attack on the House of Lords is not just destructive and ill thought out but dangerous too.

There are plenty of good arguments in favour of the House of Lords staying as it is and it is a sign of the Tories' current gutless cowardice that they have decided to retreat without a proper fight.

There is one argument that is not just good but vital, and I am baffled that we have not heard about it. It rests on Section 2 of the 1911 Parliament Act, which left the key to dictatorship in the hands of the Lords, because they were seen as safe guardians of freedom.

It is this: the House of Commons cannot vote to extend its life beyond five years unless the Lords agree. It is one of the central clauses in our Constitution, a guarantee against arbitrary power.

Now that MPs are more and more the paid employees of the Government and less and less free and independent representatives of the voters, this suddenly becomes important. If the Lords and the Commons both become Chambers of Toadies, doing the bidding of Downing Street, the Prime Minister will quietly gain the sort of power that dictators yearn for.

If he wants to he will be able to postpone elections. Of course we can rely on sweet Mr Blair never to do such a thing. But in the uncertain world that lies ahead, can we rely on every and any person who ever occupies Downing Street? I am not that trusting.

And then there is the attack on the principle of inheritance, which the Tories stupidly refuse to defend. Don't they realise that freedom and civilisation *depend* on inheritance? Without it, there could be no families, no property, no continuity. It is perfectly sensible for a free country to enshrine it in its constitution. But there is a more important point, which Mr Blair never answers.

If we cannot have inherited seats in the Lords, how can we have an inherited monarchy? The answer is that we can't. The PM may be too dim to spot the logic of this and will probably be surprised when he finds himself attacking the Throne, but many of his allies and advisers know perfectly well what they are doing. They realise that with the Lords abolished, the last line of defence which protects the Crown is overthrown. How safe will the Queen be then?

Not very. For, like the Lords, she retains crucial powers. She appoints Prime Ministers and dissolves Parliament. If these levers were in the hands of a toady President, Downing Street would be as powerful as Hitler's Reich Chancellery. For more than a century, British freedom has relied on the fact that our politicians were gentlemen who accepted the rules of the game. Unlike the USA whose supremely cynical Bill of Rights bars the government from becoming too powerful, we have hardly any legal restraints on our rulers.

The radicals behind the Blair project want there to be even fewer restrictions on their power. We are heading into strange and unfamiliar territory and the behaviour of this Government since it came to office has shown that it has no great love for our ancient freedoms.

Now is the time to stand up for our Constitution and the Tories will be worse than fools if they miss the chance.

19/10/98

Scrap this nasty law

Do you remember Parliament being recalled to pass special "tough" laws to deal with the Omagh bombers? Those laws, disgraceful attacks on liberty, were supposed to be vital to round up the evil men responsible for the outrage – though not the evil men who are now our partners in the "peace process".

Well, no evil men seem to have been rounded up, on either side of the border. So can we please have another emergency session of Parliament to repeal this shameful Act? Otherwise, people might suspect it was passed just to take away our freedom.

7/12/98

ULSTER

Gunmen will set sights on Dublin rule

We have been bombed into yesterday's surrender and, as a result, we will now be blackmailed into many further retreats until Ulster is ruled from Dublin. British democracy has sustained a total and unmitigated defeat which has cracked the foundations of the State.

The hijacking of the word "peace" by the agreement's supporters should not blind us to the truth. Murderous violence, which never stopped, will not now end as by magic, for it has just been rewarded handsomely.

Even if this were not so, an ancient war such as this cannot be settled by a cloudy form of words and a few compromises. What we have in Northern Ireland is a classic ethnic conflict – two rival groups, neither willing to be ruled by the other. Nowhere has human genius found any permanent and civilised solution to such rivalry.

So, while the signing of yesterday's piece of paper is an achievement of diplomacy, the fruit of great technical skill, patience and hard work, it must be tested against reality.

The worm in the rose is the original sin of the whole project. It was designed to appease the demands of the IRA. Just as dangerous, it is also meant to buy off the Protestant murder gangs.

To do this, it must outrage the promises given by British political leaders for three decades that they would "never give in to terror". People who cheer today will be shocked tomorrow at how swiftly the most revolting killers are released from their guarded guest-house at the Maze.

Meantime, the front-line of combat against terror, the Royal

Ulster Constabulary, will be subjected to a politically correct inquisition designed to make it "acceptable" to nationalists – that is, ineffective against the IRA.

These measures will be for good. They will destroy any idea that the British Government is ready to use force and authority to combat the IRA. But the political parts of the deal will not be so lasting. The Ulster Assembly must castrate itself as its first political act. It will set up the real new government of Ulster, a cross-border authority which gives Dublin ministers power to intervene in the province's affairs.

And if "progress" towards unity is too slow the "Continuity IRA", or some other subsidiary of Sinn Fein, can let off a bomb, or leave one lying around. Sinn Fein only supports the agreement as a station on the way to its final, fascist goal.

The mooring ropes which bind Northern Ireland to the UK will be loosened, then untied and a slow drift towards Dublin rule will begin.

What could go wrong? Well, what would you describe as wrong, when the whole thing is an insult to democracy, law and justice?

The people of Northern Ireland could reject this imposed peace at a referendum. The people of the Republic could torpedo the plan by refusing to vote to change their constitution.

The Unionist Party could split asunder ousting Mr David Trimble for signing a document which defies its whole purpose.

What we have signed up to is further ethnic cleansing of Protestants from the West of Ulster, rising power of intimidation and protection rackets in the terrorists' enclaves, internecine assassinations, a big bomb in London to hurry things along, A quiet flight of educated and prosperous Protestants, and continued beatings and murders by IRA or UVF gangsters.

11/4/98

Sick bags ready for grisly Gerry

Have your anti-nausea pills ready for Thursday's visit by the gruesome Mr Gerry Adams to Downing Street, where he will politely tell the Prime Minister to get out of Ulster or else.

This is Mr Adams's negotiating style. Each time he has been allowed into the presence of democratic ministers, he has said more or less the same thing: "I hope you're the last British minister to have any control over Northern Ireland." Why shouldn't he act in this boorish bullying and crude manner? It worked for Hitler, when he was pushing Neville Chamberlain around, and it seems to be working for him.

The Irish Foreign Minister has already admitted that the planned new all-Ireland cross-border authority, the heart of the "peace talks", will be much like a government. He has since been forced to retract this – but only because it was true. Once the two men have had their concealed handshake, and the appeasement is over for the day, perhaps they can have a grinning contest as they stroll through the Downing Street garden, looking for traces of IRA mortar shells.

The Premier's grin is bigger, but it lacks Gerry's deadly coffin-plate gleam.

8/12/97

The Ulster Appeasement process continues on its disgusting way. The Irish journalist Kevin Myers, one of few in that country prepared to tell the truth about this, points out that there is now an official price list for murder. If your terror group kills, then your mouthpieces are excluded from the "peace talks" for six weeks. If you concentrate several killings in a few days you can have them for the same price in a bargain deal. Does this mean that if the IRA lets loose a holocaust of bombs in London, Tough Tony will keep Gerry Adams out of the talks for a whole three months?

Warning, the following paragraph may contain sarcasm:

How the IRA's leaders must tremble at the thought of such a punishment. How they must respect the muscular resolve of Mr Blair.

2/2/98

Once again, let me urge that Britain should apologise for the Bloody Sunday killings in Londonderry. But *not* as a grovelling attempt to suck up to terror.

Any apology can only be justified as an acknowledgement that Her Majesty's Roman Catholic subjects deserve the fairness and justice owed to all UK citizens.

And UK citizens they should remain, for good. It is continuing doubt about the future of Northern Ireland that keeps the terrorist murderers in business. End that doubt now with a declaration that the future of Ulster is British.

26/1/98

A few weeks ago, I accurately predicted the course of the Ulster surrender talks. Now I make another prediction. The IRA will keep their bombs and guns, and Sinn Fein will get seats in the new Ulster government.

The whole deal is based not on peace, but on the British government's cowardly fear of terror. Whenever the IRA has threatened an end to its ceasefire, London has caved in.

Now that we have debauched the justice system, opened the jails, betrayed our loyal and peaceful fellow citizens and begun to disband our military and police forces, we can hardly rediscover our lost principles.

But how embarrassing and inconvenient of the IRA to issue a reminder that it has this once-great nation on the run.

How Argentina must wish it had waited for the era of New Labour to seize the Falklands. If one more commentator compares Mr Blair to Mrs Thatcher, I think I shall throw up.

Our ex-CND Prime Minister makes Ethelred the Unready look like Winston Churchill.

4/5/98

Last night, a grim-faced Prime Minister emerged from Downing Street and issued this warning to the IRA and Sinn Fein: "Any new conditions are unacceptable. Compliance with the Belfast agreement must be absolute. The Sinn Fein resumption of compliance must be immediate and unconditional. There must be no further conditions, no negotiation, no more amendment of what was agreed."

He said the Sinn Fein leaders were "not men to be trusted", adding: "We all know, too, that it's only the threat of force that has ever allowed us to achieve any of our objectives in respect to them."

Actually I made all that up. Mr Blair did not direct these threats at the people who have supported a murderous and destructive bombing campaign on the British mainland, and who have praised the attempted assassination of Margaret Thatcher as "a blow for democracy".

Instead, he aimed them at an unpleasant dictator 2,000 miles away who presents no current threat to this country but provides a convenient hate object for the embarrassing trouser-dropper who clings to the White House because he has nowhere else to go.

It is amusing, by the way, to see Bill Clinton's adviser Sandy Berger fulminating "toughly" against Saddam. I remember Mr Berger lecturing me in our Washington embassy on how the policy of weakly giving in to the IRA was so wise and far-sighted.

Mr Blair does not insist on enforcement of the agreement he sold to the British and Ulster people last Easter because he knows it is the most worthless document signed by a British Premier since Munich in 1938. It obliges him to release hundreds of killers and bombers, yet commits the IRA to precisely nothing. As I point out almost weekly, Sinn Fein did not even sign it.

Had it done so, it would have made little difference. The parts of the agreement which deal with IRA disarmament are weak and washy. The parts which deal with the release of the boys in the balaclavas are clear and unambiguous.

So, as he acted like a tinpot Churchill on Saturday night, Mr Blair knew that his personal policy had secured the release of 204 terrorists, many of them skilled bomb-makers. The arsenals of guns and explosives they once used are still untouched. How dare he pose as resolute? How dare he even think of risking the lives of British servicemen to support such a pose?

16/11/98

Most of Ulster's Protestants no longer support the so-called Good Friday Agreement, according to the latest poll.

I do not blame them. They were the victims of high-pressure salesmanship by Princess Tony and they have found out that the shiny package contained stinking fish.

There is nothing they can do about it. The referendum, Princess Tony's favourite ploy for bypassing and bullying Parliament, cannot be held again. Unlike an ordinary Act of Parliament, it cannot be repealed, a grave change to the British constitution.

If later on the people of Scotland, Wales and London discover that the things they voted for are not quite what they seemed, they too will be stuck with a decision made in haste.

What is worse, referendums in this country are held without any rules of fairness. The BBC and the rest can take sides, and the Government can use its power and your money to get its way – and the Government always has the big advantage of calling for a Yes vote.

Now we are promised more and still more of these nasty one-way streets, all of them leading Britain away from the happy settled certainties of recent years and downwards towards dark dangers – mass release of convicts, break up of the UK, increased control of politics by party machines, permanent coalition government.

Personally, I would follow the example of Germany and ban them. But if we can't do that, Parliament *must* pass laws to make them fair.

8/3/99

It wasn't a Good Friday after all

Just over a year ago, the commentators of Fleet Street gave their verdict on the Northern Ireland agreement. All but one – me – approved of it. I invite the others to look up the files and see what they wrote, and ask them if they now feel they were deceived.

I admit that I underestimated the ability of the Government to persuade Ulster Protestants to vote for such a flawed deal, though many now wish they hadn't. However, I stand by the following, written on April 10, 1998: "People who cheer today will be shocked tomorrow at how swiftly the most revolting killers are released.

"Murderous violence, which never stopped, will not now end as by magic, because it has just been rewarded handsomely.

"The front-line of combat against terror, the RUC, will be subjected to a politically-correct inquisition designed to make it 'acceptable' to nationalists, that is, ineffective against the IRA."

I also warned of "continued beatings and murders by IRA or UVF gangsters".

As the Prime Minister and Dr Mowlam flounder about, trying to conceal the chasm at the heart of this low, dishonest deal, will they at least admit the possibility that their chosen road of surrender to terror is not necessarily the only, or even the best, route to peace?

19/4/99

The bitter price of surrender

Has Mr Christopher Patten started to enjoy hauling down the Union Jack? He seemed sad enough, tearful even, as the emblem of British justice and liberty was folded up and put away for ever in Hong Kong.

Now Mr Patten is strangely dry-eyed as he strips the symbols of Britishness from the Royal Ulster Constabulary. Looking all noble and brisk, he says the RUC should be "free from any association with the British and Irish States".

Excuse me? I nipped upstairs when I read this and looked at my passport. That miserable Euro-document is a melancholy reminder of better days, but it still says that our country is called the United Kingdom of Great Britain and Northern Ireland.

So why exactly is it that policemen in this country should be "freed" from their association with Britain? What now are they defending with their lives? What law? What justice? What freedom?

This report, accepted with amazing speed by Mr Blair's anti-British Government, is not really about the police at all. It is an act of surrender, following directly from the shameful defeat inflicted upon this country thanks to the unsigned treaty we made with the IRA on Good Friday 1998.

Worse, it is done solely to please the IRA. While they will not be satisfied until the whole of the RUC is dissolved, they are happy enough with this grave blow to its morale and purpose, though they are not fools enough to say so.

They grasp the importance of these things. They know that the harp, crown and shamrock intertwined on the RUC badge are the symbol of the idea they most hate – that it is possible for a Catholic Irishman to be a loyal subject of the Queen. They are enraged that any Catholic should join the RUC. Their tactics have taken cynicism to new depths.

First of all, they murdered, or threatened to murder, the

fantastically brave Catholics who have joined that force. They have used other despicable methods to stop Catholics signing up in the first place.

Then, they whined that there were not enough Catholics in it, having bloodily made sure that this was so.

The rightful response of a "civilised" man, which Mr Patten is always claiming to be, would be to crush, imprison and disband the cynical terror mafias. But our "civilised" establishment is now so feeble and unpatriotic that it would rather undermine the RUC than disarm the IRA.

This is the trouble with "peace". I still meet people who insist that the current state of affairs in Ulster is better than the alternative. This is only true on the most base calculation of profit and loss.

Peace without victory is a downward stairway. As Winston Churchill said, it starts broad and well-lit but rapidly grows darker, narrower and steeper.

Had we made peace with Hitler 60 years ago, as some "civilised" politicians urged at the time, there would have been plenty of benefits: no bombs going off in London (sound familiar?). No conscription. Lower taxes. No rationing or evacuation.

But bit by bit the truth would come home. First, the scrapping or handover of the Fleet and the RAF. Then the censoring of the press and BBC so as not to offend Berlin.

Then the pressure, steadily growing, from a confident enemy, ending perhaps with the shameful transport of British Jews to an unspeakable death in the East. And all the while, the soothing voices purring that at least there was no war. Sometimes, and often in the history of this country, war has been better than peace. My disgust and shame for what is being done to the RUC is too great for words alone to express.

If they can do it to the RUC, how long before they abandon you too to lawlessness and evil? Protest while you can.

13/9/99

134

The making of this very modern saint

Call no man happy until he is dead, and call no man a saint until the cold judges of history have had time to weigh him in the balance without love or hate but with justice.

It is time to halt the flow of gush and hushed reverence for Nelson Mandela, a remarkable but flawed man who is, ultimately, a politician and, therefore, subject to the same rules as the rest of them.

Even the South African President himself may be feeling a little impatient with the oceans of sycophantic drivel which slosh about his feet as he makes his royal progress through London.

Certainly, if he is half the man he is made out to be, he must wince in private at the way in which he has been installed on his own personal cloud by a simpering choir of commentators.

Nobody dares ask him hard questions about the dubious nature of his country. Nor is he attacked in public for his growing detachment from the machinery of government which, according to Cape Town rumour, is very much like the declining years of Ronald Reagan's rule in Washington. Instead, we are treated to the sort of sentimental tosh used throughout the ages to gild figureheads and dictators.

We are told he actually talks to his chauffeurs and holds up banquets while he natters to kitchen staff.

Of course, Mandela has some outstanding qualities. His serenity, his ability to suffer long and be kind, his beautiful, Fifties English and his royal bearing are clean, inspiring virtues in a world of coarseness, retaliation and shouting.

But such attributes are shared by countless others now living on this Earth.

How many of us can name a single Chinese dissident out of the thousands persecuted and butchered during and after Tiananmen Square? Where are the streets named after the imprisoned or censored opponents of the many gory regimes of black Africa?

Come to that, who now even remembers Alexander Solzhenitsyn or Andrei Sakharov, the towering opponents of Soviet rule, or Anatoly Koryagin, the psychiatrist who exposed the Kremlin's ghastly treatment of dissidents and was so badly handled in the gulag that his own wife could not recognise him?

Then there is Vaclav Havel, who made a Mandela-style progress from prison to presidential palace in Prague. But he does not receive the Nelsonian halo.

Yet these men used no force against the horrific governments they faced, apart from the power of their own thoughts.

Nelson Mandela, on the other hand, actively chose the path of violence against the South African regime when many others counselled against it. He knowingly worked alongside emissaries and toadies of Soviet power who hoped to turn South Africa into a client state of the USSR. Had his cause triumphed in the days of the Cold War, their cause would have triumphed, too.

Nor has he been blameless in his personal life. His first wife Evelyn learned of his plans to divorce her through a newspaper advertisement shown to her by friends. He left her for the woman who must count as his greatest personal and political mistake, the sinister and unpleasant Winnie. So why the exaggerated and embarrassing canonisation, the stacks of honorary degrees and the suspension of disbelief? It is because the South African cause became the heart of the greatest modern secular religion: self-indulgent breast beating over the distant woes of others.

The Pretoria regime, though stupid and foul, was no more so than dozens of other governments of Left and Right which have stained the globe during the past half-century.

But it contained a number of special factors. Almost alone, South Africa refused to accept the fashionable idea that self-rule was superior to colonial government.

Its white people lived as comfortably as American whites but dwelt an embarrassingly short distance away from the exploited black poor.

There is no *moral* difference between living a Western lifestyle 8,000 miles away from Soweto, or doing the same thing 10 miles away. But all these Europeans and Americans, who felt a guilt about sharing the same planet with squalid townships, harboured a special rage against South African whites for daring to do so.

For the liberal intelligentsia, it was also comforting to have a Right-wing government that was every bit as nasty as the communist regimes which constantly embarrassed them, but which they felt they had to defend.

In Britain, this feeling was enhanced by the century-old rivalry between mainly liberal, English-speaking settlers in the Cape and the iron-hard, racialist Afrikaners.

In America, South Africa was an easy target for the flagging civil rights movement, which has failed to end the informal apartheid which divides most major cities in the USA. So it became especially important that, out of all the unacceptable states on Earth, South Africa should be made to fall.

In their hearts, those who have brought this about know perfectly well that they have not done much (if any) good to the black majority.

Without exception, black African states have slid into corruption, lawlessness and confusion within a few short years of independence.

There is no real reason to suppose that South Africa will be any different, apart from wishful thinking.

That is why Nelson Mandela's personal qualities are exaggerated in this laughable way – to draw attention away from the faults of his country and the squalor of the political machine which waits behind him.

He provides a fig-leaf to cover this up and to create a secular myth that the "new" South Africa is some sort of unique heaven on earth, where the lion lies down with the lamb and the Earth shall be full of the knowledge of the Lord as the waters cover the sea.

If only it could be so.

10/7/96

England and Scotland should get ready for a nasty divorce

Goodbye, Scotland. I for one shall be sorry to see you go. My earliest memories are of Scottish voices and Scottish landscapes and I had always thought we were two equal peoples in one country.

I never doubted that Scotland had brought great gifts to the union – especially scholarship and valour. The giant achievements of Britain in the past three centuries would have been impossible without Scotland's almost incredible concentration of talent.

We work well together – Matthew Boulton and James Watt, Samuel Johnson and James Boswell. And good humour and restraint have allowed us to live happily in each other's territory. I hope we still can.

But in this age of silly, spiteful, unstoppable divorces there is nothing that we can do to get you back and you should now prepare yourself for a series of increasingly nasty disputes about power, property and money. Without our subsidy, Scotland would have to raise the basic tax rate not by three pence in the pound but by 40 pence in the pound.

Now that there is to be a parliament in Edinburgh, the number of Scottish MPs at Westminster should drop from 72 to 41 and even they should really abstain on English issues.

But Tony Blair will not cut the subsidy, or seriously reduce the MPs. And out of this will grow a slow but unstoppable English resentment which will push the two countries apart – and eventually drive a nominally independent Scotland into the arms of a rival lover and paymaster, the European Union.

Scots deluded by *Braveheart* who think that they have struck a blow for their culture should look at what Brussels has done to Ireland in a few short years. It may be richer but it is far, far less Irish.

Scots will find, as plenty of others have done, that there are many worse people in this world than the English they currently despise.

What a sorry, needless shame this has all been.

15/9/97

Why should the Germans now pretend that Britain had only a minor role in the 1948 Berlin Airlift, that moving act of determination, generosity and courage that may well have saved Europe from Soviet tyranny?

Out of 77 who died in the perilous and exhausting operation 40 were British.

The RAF operated eight of the 12 airfields and supplied nearly half the food.

Yet official German publications barely mention the British effort and wrongly say that Britain only joined in "later", after the Americans.

I suspect this is part of a wider rewriting of European history, in which Britain's unique past will be forgotten or minimised, because it reminds our "partners" of their folly in electing Hitler or their shame in collaborating with him. The Airlift underlines the fact that a victorious Britain was still a great power in 1948.

Anything which highlights our different history and traditions must be quietly forgotten. But help from the USA can be admitted because they are not part of Europe.

26/1/98

Goofy geeks are too young to be Tories

How sad that the Young Tories, that great middle-class wedding bureau, are to be wound up. I think the trouble was that they forgot their real purpose and started talking about politics. Young people really shouldn't *be* Tories. Tory youngsters all too often turn out to be geeks with goofy teeth and all their buttons done up too tightly.

On the other hand, middle-aged and old people shouldn't be socialists. It is a sign of refusing to grow up, like having grey hair and wearing jeans at the same time.

26/1/98

Year by year, our MPs defy the true feelings of the country, through the same sneaky, dishonest and misnamed trick. It is called the "free vote", and is now to be used to make it legal for homosexual predators to recruit ignorant and impressionable 16-year-olds to their sad, seedy dead-end of a world.

What is "free" about these votes? Far from being free, they invariably do the bidding of whatever is fashionable, liberal opinion in a few North London postal districts.

Such "free" votes almost always scornfully ignore the feelings of most sensible, experienced people who fear for their children and for the morality and stability of the country. But the important thing about these decisions is that neither of the two major political parties needs to take responsibility for them at a general election. And this is despite the fact that they have a giant effect on our lives.

Who do we blame for the mass slaughter of the abortion clinics? It was a free vote, squire. Who do we blame for the fact that killing a human being means about six years in jail? It was a free vote, guv.

Who do we blame for the fact that it is easier to get a

divorce than it is to get a new passport? Not us, sorry, that was a free vote, too. Who will we be able to blame when dope is legalised and crime turns from epidemic to pandemic? You can bet that will be a free vote as well. Part of the point of democracy is that you always know who to blame when things go wrong, and then punish them at the polls.

I don't care if Tony Blair is a Catholic or a Protestant or a Zen Buddhist. That's his business. All I want to know is whether he and his party plan to strengthen traditional morality or to carry on wrecking it. The same goes for William Hague and his friends.

9/3/98

A year ago I wrote that the Tories were finished. I see no reason to change my mind. British parliamentary democracy, which relies on strong opposition, died and was laid to rest on May 1, 1997. Now we shall see the completion of the British cultural revolution, which will bury the things we once valued. Nobody under 30 knows any history. Few are familiar with the mighty role we played in keeping Europe and the world free, and in spreading law, liberty and civilisation across the globe. Those who are still proud of this record are openly mocked, as was the MP Peter Tapsell in the Commons last week

The great pillars of our language and literature moulder unread. Nobody reads our poets any more, or learns their lines. Some of our heritage has been suppressed, as the King James Bible and the 1662 Prayer Book have been by a Church which hates their hard truths.

The gentleness, self-control and independence of mind that went with this culture have all withered too.

All that is left is the moronic inferno of self-indulgence, licence and noise, known as Cool Britannia, where slavish conformism is rewarded and free speech is feared.

4/5/98

Sports Minister Tony Banks has explained why he would not debate with me on Radio 4's *Any Questions*. He says that I am "an objectionable lout and a bar-room bully".

Ouch. I feel as if I have been savaged by a dead sheep.

I imagine it would feel much the same as being called "long-winded" by Neil Kinnock, "shifty" by Richard Nixon or "inflexible" by Dr Ian Paisley.

15/6/98

Margaret Thatcher failed. Britain now has more nationalised industries than ever before and they are the wrong ones.

After the barmy privatisation of the railways by our last Prime Minister, whose name I forget, we now face a lunatic auction of the air-traffic control system and of a number of other things which are either unsaleable or best left in state hands.

The money raised, if any, will be poured into our vast new state sector, the National Illiteracy Corporation, which runs the education industry, the National Nagging Service of social workers, health education busybodies etc and the National Hypochondria Service with its exciting new league tables of death.

All of them are expensive failures run for the benefit of their employees, who now vastly outnumber the ranks of the Soviet Army at the height of the Cold War.

Government cash, which is mostly money confiscated from you and me under pain of imprisonment, will also be tipped into that other great black hole of waste, bureaucracy and sleaze: the local authorities.

And it will flow into the Labour Party's great pet project, the nationalisation of childhood. If current policies are effective, almost every child over the age of three (and many well below this age) will soon be brought up by paid strangers rather than by their own parents.

The old nationalised industries did at least have to produce something – steel, coal, ships, gas, electricity, phone services –

which people wanted and were willing to pay for. True, they often did it badly and it was discontent over their performance which helped the Tories to power in 1979.

But amid the squabbles and shrill arguments over their sell-off, people failed to notice that a new and more important state sector was growing up, which produces almost nothing except statistics, bogus qualifications, dubious league tables and vast unfunded pension commitments.

It is here that Labour now finds its main strength. It was for them that Gordon Brown was speaking when he staged his putsch against Tony Blair on Thursday, a putsch which the Prime Minister did not really understand and which a football-obsessed nation has barely noticed.

Mr Brown plans a vast increase in state spending, up by two and three-quarters per cent per year, and a terrifying rise in taxation, up by £8 billion per year.

You have already found out that Nice New Labour wants to break up the United Kingdom. Now it is time to discover its other, more traditional purpose – tax and waste.

15/6/98

Toady or not toady…?

Two weeks ago, I brought you the strange story of the senior civil servant said to have lavished nauseating praise on the Prime Minister. The Cabinet Secretary, Sir Richard Wilson, was reported by a reputable Labour journalist as having said that Mr Blair was "The most courageous politician I have ever met." The remark was allegedly made at a time and place when it was likely to be heard by outsiders.

Sir Richard's office denied that he had said these toadying words and assured me he would write to the *Evening Standard* (which printed the story) to put the record straight. I have a shorthand note (though not a tape recording) of this assurance.

However, Sir Richard's office now claim they didn't say this, so they obviously can't have done, and my note must be wrong because our civil service has an enviable record for accuracy. There will be no letter to the *Standard*, only one to the journalist.

It's a good thing they never did say what I thought they said. It would have been rather hard for the Cabinet Secretary to write to the papers and say: "Tony Blair ISN'T the most courageous politician I have ever met." Oh dear, oh dear, what a mess I seem to have caused.

13/7/98

Mr Gordon Brown is now the Prime Minister of this country in all but name and the pitiful Tony Blair merely a simpering figurehead. Mr Brown was always the cleverer and sharper of the two younger Scotsmen who fought to take over the defeated remnants of the Labour Party. Now he has proved it.

Mr Blair was never what he was cracked up to be. The truth is that he is a rather ignorant, bad-tempered man with a certain charm and a good TV presence but without two thoughts to rub together, or any grasp of detail.

Try reading one of his cloudy, over-praised speeches and see if you can detect a single solid idea in it.

He took the credit for breaking the power of the unions over the Labour Party – after Margaret Thatcher and Norman Tebbit had done the real hard work for him.

But in reality he was created from nothing by Labour's establishment, angry that the silly antics of the wild Left had kept them out of power for years and badly in need of an acceptable face to front their unacceptable return to power.

They wanted to slash our defences, break up the UK and merge the remains in a European superstate – so it helped to have Mr Blair, who looked and sounded like a patriot.

They wanted to stop state schools breaking away from the power of town hall commissars – so it helped to have Mr Blair with his plausible blather about "education". But above all they wanted to raise taxes and go back to the stupid old days when enterprise was punished and milked to pay for the wasteful and useless public sector where most Labour supporters work.

Now they've nearly done all three. Mr Blair himself, surrounded by lightweights, influence-peddlers, flatterers and toadies, is still barely aware that he presides over one of the most Left-wing governments in British history, though he looked pretty twitchy as he sat beside Mr Brown during his Tuesday speech.

He will be allowed to prance about on the world stage just as long as he does not get in the way of Gordon Brown's people's government. He is Mr Brown's human shield, his personal popularity hiding the unpopularity of Labour's policies.

A fawning media, mostly from the same shallow know-nothing culture that produced Tony Blair, have also failed to recognise what is taking place before their eyes. But Mr Brown's coup d'etat last week thrust the truth in all our faces. He spends first and asks questions afterwards and ministers who do not obey him will be punished.

We have not had such firm government since Lady Thatcher was chucked out of power by a bunch of cowards and pygmies. What a pity that our most effective and cunning living politician is a dogmatic socialist, stuck in the Stone Age of thought.

20/7/98

In the end it turned out to be important that President Bill Clinton is a cheat and a liar. What a relief. I had come close to nausea as the world shrugged and made excuses for the shameful buffoon who squats pathetically in the White House this morning, his dishonoured name a joke for the rest of history.

But why was it important? Is there a connection between all those lush young ladies used and tossed aside like half-smoked cigars and the handshakes with the apostles of murder that we had to witness last week in Ulster?

Actually, yes, there is. Mr Clinton is the standard bearer of easy morals in private and public life, welcomed to the White House by millions because they felt at last they were in power, too.

Here at last was a US president who could really tap his toes, a funky sex and drugs and rock and roll president, in tune with the most self-centred, pampered and spoiled generation in modern history.

He winked at dope, he despised the military but, above all, he was not bothered about sexual morality. On the contrary, he was pledged to preserve that great Charter of Rights for the selfish libertines of both sexes, abortion on demand.

The killing of unborn babies is the key to Clinton. He knew that this policy had turned off millions of working-class Catholic voters but he also knew how much it mattered to his friends.

So he discovered Ireland. By giving his backing to the Irish nationalist cause, he won back many of those votes – which just happen to be concentrated in those states which are useful to have on your side if you want to win a presidential election.

There is no evidence that Bill Clinton ever cared about Ulster before, nor that he knew anything about it. He left all that side of things to Teddy Kennedy, another creature of low morals, whose bimbos have an even tougher time than President Clinton's.

Helped along by the weakness and lack of principle of the last Tory premier, The Jelly, he was able to use Belfast as a photo opportunity for the 1996 presidential election.

Encouraged by the slavishness of the new Labour premier, the Pixie, he hoped to use Omagh in the same way, to obliterate the face of Monica Lewinski from the TV screens, to exploit Ireland much as he exploited Monica herself.

Well, he has failed and, with any luck, will soon be kicked

into retirement whining and lying and still refusing to admit that he has done anything wrong. At least he will be able to play golf with O. J. Simpson – if Mr Simpson doesn't mind being seen with him.

And meanwhile the law-abiding and peaceful people of Northern Ireland will have to get used to a world in which Martin McGuinness, yes, Martin McGuinness, is viewed as a statesman.

7/9/98

The United States will be damaged to its heart

Whenever I try optimism, I quickly regret it. I wrote last week that morals had turned out to matter after all, as it seemed that President Clinton was at last being forced to face his own great wickedness.

It is already clear that I was taken in by a carefully-timed exercise in advance damage control. Mr Clinton and his allies do not actually think he has done anything seriously wrong and he is just going through the motions of sorrow to deflect the anger of the old-fashioned and the honest.

It is plain that resignation has never crossed his mind. He will not leave the White House unless he is dragged from it, with his fingernails scraping along Pennsylvania Avenue.

But who will drag him? I suspect nobody will. Those with the power to do so – the American media and the Washington political establishment – suffer from the same moral disorders as he does and so will never launch the merciless attack needed to dislodge him.

So, believing that it is my job to risk the occasional prediction even if it is dragged up and used against me for years to come, I now prophesy that, many months hence, Congress will pass a vote of censure against the President to which he will respond with a penitent look and a brief speech admitting that he has been bad but has now stopped and will try again, as he once said to his pal Dick Morris, to "shut his body down sexually". Though, of course, he may slip up again. He will then pretend that he is busy (the truth is that he has practically nothing to do except watch movies and play golf) and adopt his serious statesman expression.

And that will be that, except that the United States of America will be damaged to its heart and will never recover. A nation of free men cannot long survive unless they govern that freedom with an unbending code of morals. That code, long under attack, is now fatally weakened.

The obligation to tell the truth with candour will be watered down. Instead, nobody will expect any more than selective, self-serving accuracy, if that.

And the duty to keep the law will be blurred. Instead of a law that arches above the heads of all citizens, Americans will have a law which successful people do not have to obey, especially if they think it is interfering with their private lives.

These are the new principles established by Mr Clinton's escape. Beside them is a new gospel, which offers forgiveness to those who can weep to order and feign all the other outward signs of contrition, without having paid any real price.

As for shame, I think we can confidently work on the assumption that it has been abolished.

For if it still existed, Mr Clinton would be begging the lovely hills of the Virginia Blue Ridge to fall upon him and hide him from the sight of his fellow men. Instead he parades in public with a fat smile on his corrupt face.

14/9/98

I enjoyed the Cold War, a rare patch of sanity when the democracies ignored pacifist propaganda and faced down their enemies with confidence and strength. But I am not enjoying the new TV series about it, which is trite, CND-ish and soft on the

Soviet Union. I rather suspect that next week's episode will come up with the stupid old idea that the USSR was only trying to defend itself from the West when it enslaved much of Europe.

Stalin did not sign his pact with Hitler to "buy time", as the programme suggested. He signed it to seize half of Poland, a chunk of Romania and all three Baltic states. If he was buying time, why was he so hopelessly unprepared for war when it came in 1941?

And if they have such good access to archives, why didn't the makers find pictures (printed in the Nazi book *Sieg in Polen*) of the joint Nazi–Soviet victory parade held in Brest, Poland, in October 1940? Or documents about the well-known exchanges of prisoners between the Gestapo and the Soviet NKVD secret police? And why have they accepted the vastly inflated Soviet casualty figures for the war, which almost certainly include millions murdered in Soviet concentration camps?

They also seem not to have read the excellent *History of Europe* by Norman Davies, which debunks the myth that the Western allies "intervened" to crush the Russian revolution in 1917. If only they had.

21/9/98

There was something very nasty about the behaviour of Britain's media in Bournemouth last week. It's not that I'm against journalists giving politicians a rough time, I'm all for it. Mockery and criticism are good for powerful men and women.

But stop a moment. Many of the papers and programmes and people who lashed and smashed the Tories were the same ones who coated the Labour conference in flattery and toadying praise just the week before.

Isn't it creepy when the Press, and especially the tax-funded BBC, grovel to the Government and attack the Opposition?

I remember another conference at Bournemouth, a Labour one, where Neil Kinnock won a largely phoney confrontation with the pimple-sized Militant Tendency. I remember when Tony Blair abolished the outdated Clause Four of the Labour constitution. Both times, Labour Opposition leaders were praised for their statesmanship and toughness, not damned for splitting their parties, though they did so on each occasion.

But when William Hague took a much larger risk and overwhelmingly faced down the extremists Kenneth Clarke and Michael Heseltine, the Fourth Estate portrayed the event as a party split down the middle (well, split 84 per cent to 16 per cent, since you ask).

It largely ignored the growing unpopularity of Heseltine, an ill old man who, I'm told, was booed by former supporters at one private gathering. And it pumped up the supposed "threat" to Hague from the absurd, overrated Michael Portillo, who may be about to get his own show on some leftist TV station but is not even an MP. He is nothing like as great a threat to Hague as Gordon Brown is to Tony Blair but you wouldn't know it from last week's coverage, especially on the BBC.

A democracy needs an opposition and it needs a free media – and they both need each other to survive. Unless members of my trade want to become the neutered lapdogs of a permanent Labour government, they should relearn the difficult art of attacking the people who have power, rather than those who have none.

5/10/98

Shining palace for toady MPs

The transformation of the House of Commons into a privileged neutered Supreme Soviet goes on apace. MPs can't have consciences or independent views these days, but they've *got* to have offices.

It helps to keep them out of the Commons chamber where

they might actually remember what they were elected to do.

And their new People's Palace is now rising at Westminster, with two ornamental pools, a restaurant and lavish office suites. This seven-storey building is costing you and me £240 million. Of that, £34 million alone is going on a special bronze facade because it looks nicer and will last longer.

Pity I can't afford a nice bronze facade for my own crumbling semi, but there isn't enough money left after all the taxes.

Anti-royalists please note. The cost of the facade is only slightly less than the bill for the total rebuilding of the inside of Windsor Castle after its fire. Remember the fuss about that.
19/10/98

Far more important than Ron

The resignation of Ron Davies has no political importance, unless you are one of the tiny band of people who is actually gripped by Welsh politics. Yet our media devote huge resources to probing the affair.

I wish they would spend half as much effort on investigating the incredibly close result of the Welsh devolution referendum, Mr Davies's great triumph held under rules rightly criticised by Lord Neill. I am not suggesting that anything improper took place but if my country is to be broken up, I would like to be sure that the voting involved was fairly conducted.
2/11/98

UN is tyrants' friend

If the United Nations had existed in 1944, the Nazis would still be in power in Germany because the Security Council would have thought it was wrong to overthrow their regime. Weapons inspectors would be criss-crossing Germany, probably failing to find secret missile factories and nuclear plants. And we would still be applying futile sanctions, which the Nazi elite would use as an excuse for depriving their people.

The UN is the result of a soppy liberal fantasy that there is something called "International Law". In truth, the best you can hope for is that the big battalions are on the side of good.
23/11/98

Mighty British justice can detain a broken-down old dictator who came here to sort out his bad back, but somehow it can't punish burglars, car thieves, vandals, muggers, football hooligans and drunks who mow down children on the roads.

The Law Lords can hound South American despots, but haven't the spine to support the rights of English parents to decide if their under-age daughters should be fed contraceptive pills by amoral clinics.

Surely we had better justice when our judges were harder on home-grown criminals and uninterested in politics? Surely, courage, like charity, begins at home?

It is so easy to parade your conscience in other people's countries, where you don't have to live with the consequences. How fierce, how lofty, the majority Law Lords must feel, that they have struck out against Augusto Pinochet, now nothing but a husk of the torturer and murderer he used to be.

But would any of them have stood up to a real live Pinochet in their own country? I wonder.

Their decision on Thursday bowed to the British dictatorship of fashion. It is fashionable to believe in "International Law", fashionable to be passionate about Chile's undoubtedly nasty past. In the same way, the British judiciary's weakness in the face of crime is modish, linked to the crazy idea that wrongdoers should be "rehabilitated" rather than punished. And its failure to defend the family and help parents keep their children from harm also follows the current fashion, which claims that any old collection of adults and children under one roof is equal to a lifelong faithful marriage and that sex is a recreation, like tennis.

But justice is supposed to be blind to trends. In which case, what business is it of courts what foreign tyrants do in their own countries?

Perhaps, if our streets and homes were secure, and our women and old people felt happy to go out after dark, if parents did not fear constantly for their children's safety, we *might*, just *might*, have some right to interfere in faraway battles. But even then, what principle have we now cemented?

A stupid one. General Pinochet, for all his grievous faults, stepped down without a fight and handed his country back to democracy. If he had refused to do so and had hung on to office by violence and savagery, we could not have touched him however many times he came to London to take tea with Lady Thatcher.

All the many tyrants of the world will take one message from the Law Lords' ruling – that they should not give up power this side of the grave. For all those countries hoping for a release from tyranny, this must be very bad news indeed.
30/11/98

When I had stopped laughing at Peter Mandelson's resignation letter, I began to do some serious gloating. I had to interrupt the gloating briefly for the season of goodwill but now I can start again.

The epistle was funny because – like everyone who is chucked out of this Government – he insisted that he had done nothing wrong. It was only because the common herd could not understand that Mr Mandelson had a perfect right to live miles beyond his means that he was handing in his red boxes.

It was yet another sign of this Government's Marie

Antoinette complex, the one thing which might yet bring them down before it is too late. With their showy personal wealth and their snobbery of worldly success, they may eventually disgust enough voters to destroy their majority.

If they fall for this reason, I shan't be sorry. With a few decent exceptions, the Blair ministry is made up of shallow, amoral self-seekers, almost as ignorant about this country as they are about the rest of the world, scornful of liberty, out of love with truth and scared of free speech.

As for their great plan, the rushed and rigged entry of Britain into a European superstate, any peaceful, democratic means are justified in upsetting it but I would much prefer a proper old-fashioned debate in which this appalling idea could be defeated by good old reason.

28/12/98

The phoney refugees who kill compassion

The family is collapsing, the schools refuse to teach right and wrong, the churches are emptying, fewer and fewer people are marrying in church or baptizing their children.

Doctors slay 150,000 innocent but inconvenient babies a year, a total that would have impressed Herod. Dozens of parsons seem to believe in government rather than God. So what does the Archbishop of Canterbury, heir of St Augustine and the martyred Thomas Cranmer, talk about at Christmastide?

He has the gall to compare the Holy Family, who fled to Egypt to escape Herod the child-murderer, with the sordid frauds who come to this country pretending to be refugees so that they can sponge off Europe's most easily-fooled social security system.

My wife and I both have ancestors who came to Britain because they feared – rightly – what would happen to them if they stayed in Russia or Prussia. They were welcomed by this generous nation, where they found work and prospered. They did not seek or expect any housing benefit or other State dole. What they sought, and found, was tolerance and the freedom to live in peace and become British.

Thanks to the cynical abuse of the words "refugee" and "asylum" by modern migrants, it is likely that the doors of this country will soon swing shut against all comers, including genuine victims.

The sloppy, soppy thinking of the Archbishop of Canterbury will be at least partly to blame.

4/1/99

Princess Tony will never make me a People's Peer

I think we should coin a name for those Tories who have decided to fall in with Princess Tony's abolition of Britain – Collaborator Conservatives. Like some of the men of Vichy, France, they do not much like their new friends but reckon resistance is futile and that cooperation may save something from the wreckage.

No doubt Lord Wakeham hopes, by chairing the Royal Commission on the Lords, to preserve a little of the old place.

His motives are, of course, decent and honest. But bit by bit the compromises and the sad surrenders grow, until in the end the collaborators are worse than their masters.

Do not go down this road. Offer no help. This Government is not decent or fair, and will have no gratitude, only contempt, for your weakness. None of them would ever have aided a Tory government, and quite right, too.

Thanks, by the way, to the readers who nominated me as a People's Peer the other day. But I somehow think I am not quite what Princess Tony had in mind. A dim rock star or two, a naively sweet teacher, a few TV newsreaders, a gameshow host, a funky businessman (guess who?), a have-a-go hero and a politically correct copper are more in his line.

25/1/99

One Prime Minister, one vote

Some people still don't see how Princess Tony, the man who supposedly brought democracy to the Labour Party, can use the nailed club of the block vote to get his way in Wales.

Some people don't see why a premier who wants to centralise everything seems to like giving power away to "regions". Some people cannot understand the difference between "old" and new" Labour. Here is all you need to know: Princess Tony did not want democracy but control. He is quite happy to use the block vote for that when he "gives" power to Scotland and Wales; he takes it away from Parliament, which he despises. Then he hopes to run both the Scottish Parliament and the Welsh Assembly through his centralised machine. It is the same with his plans for the Lords. Life peers are no more democratic than hereditary ones, but he's keeping them because it's easier to order them about.

And the problem with old Labour wasn't that it was Left-wing. New Labour is far more Left-wing. It was that it contained people who wouldn't do what they were told by Princess Tony.

22/2/99

Hague must bin Maggie

I am sick and tired of Magaret Thatcher. Her personal gratitude to General Pinochet for his Falklands help is all very well but the man did torture and murder his political opponents, and democrats should not seek to gloss over this nasty fact.

Why does she go and pay a state visit to him? It is another piece of flawed judgement, though not nearly as bad as when she let it be put about that she thought highly of Princess Tony, the man who is now burying most of her achievements.

If William Hague wants to have any hope of winning the next election — and if he loses, the Tories are doomed — he must grasp that the Thatcher years were in many ways a missed opportunity. She failed to save the schools or the universities from the levellers. She ravaged the BBC with accountants but did nothing to bring back its moral power or its impartiality. She was bamboozled by civil servants, colleagues and diplomats over Europe and Ulster.

She left Britain with more state-controlled industries than when she started, the vast tax-financed empires of the NHS, local government and its quangos. And she did nothing to help the married family.

She had — and still has — many fine qualities. But in several ways she prepared the ground for this Labour government. Time to move on.

29/3/99

William Hague will not be saved by a haircut, a new suit, a voice coach or a kitchen table. His salvation lies in grasping that this government, like a playground bully, is not as popular as it thinks it is. It just needs someone to stand up to it, with principle and courage.

Labour plans to sell us to Brussels. It is grovelling to terror in Ulster. It is besmirching our national honour with its unhinged Balkan adventure.

David Blunkett is the worst Education Secretary in memory. The Deputy Prime Minister is so arrogant that he dares to enter the Commons chamber without even bothering to brief himself on the great issues facing the nation.

Have no mercy on this circus of anti-British phonies and clowns. Attack, attack and again attack. Chuck out the faint hearts. Expel anyone who takes a job from the enemy. It is the last chance you will get, for if Labour win the next election they will not just move the goalposts. They will move the whole stadium.

19/4/99

Chuck out those pinstripes now

There should be great bonfires of pinstriped suits on the hilltops of the nation, now that the Tories have been warned by their spin doctors not to wear them any more. This seems to me to be very sensible advice. Pinstriped suits, like baseball caps worn backwards, say in a loud voice: "I don't care what you think about me."

This may be all right for the defiantly fogeyish and for people who take pride in wearing clothes originally built for their grandfathers. Good luck to them.

But the problem for the Tories is they have stopped reproducing. No new, young Tories are being born or brought up. That's not to say they should grovel to the young, who despise such behaviour. Wearing forward-facing baseball caps and trying to be funky will not work, because it's so obviously phoney.

But if they are to become – as they must – the resistance to Princess Tony's horrible new regime, then they have at least to stop being positively repulsive. Then they can appeal to the sort of people who think that a Conservative is something you spread on your toast.

I stole the toast joke from William Hague, whose sharp sense of humour is one of the many strengths unknown to millions. It is an interesting sidelight on the constant belittling of Mr Hague by the media that he is one of the very few people who actually looks larger in real life than he does on

TV. He is almost 6ft tall and if Tony Blair ever goes bald (which I would say is not impossible) there'll only be about half an inch between them.

7/6/99

Not such a loony at all

I was saddened, but not terribly surprised, at the news that Screaming Lord Sutch was dead. Whenever I met him at by-elections, he had a kind of pale desperation about him. He may also have been puzzled that policies he picked for their crazy stupidity – votes for teenagers, honours for pop stars and all day drinking – were enacted by supposedly serious statesmen.

21/6/99

Yet again, William Hague shows himself as an astute and cunning politician, superior in every way to Princess Tony.

Compare and contrast. The Princess appears on *Question Time* and suddenly seems to commit himself to a ban on fox-hunting.

He gives the impression that he voted for the ban the first time around, saying that "people like myelf" did so. In fact, he didn't turn up. He speaks throughout in a fake cool accent, pandering to fashionable London.

William Hague, trying to cope with the rash creation of parliament for everyone except the English, suggests in a literate speech that Welsh and Scottish MPs should be barred from voting on purely English matters. Quite right. Why should some Scottish Marxist or some Leveller from the valleys be able to help abolish grammar schools in Rochester when the MP for Rochester has no say over schools in Cardiff or Elgin?

It is a great issue of our time. It needs an answer and Mr

Hague's is a good one. But can we debate it? No, everyone's obsessed with the state of the Tory treasurer's shirt buttons and the internal politics of Belize.

19/7/99

A Cabinet of puppets on their strings

Since we don't have a real government, it's hardly surprising that there was no need for a real reshuffle. Princess Tony is running a campaign, not running the country. The Cabinet is a mere puppet show, a collection of men and women paid to pretend that they are in charge.

None of these "ministers" has any real independence of action. Each is told what to do by a central command in Downing Street, which does not change and which is headed by Mr Alastair Campbell, the Prime Minister's press secretary and mental valet. Their purse strings are held tightly by Gordon Brown's Treasury, which ensures that none of them can take any serious steps without approval on high.

Why was an aircraft carrier sent to the Adriatic in the middle of the Kosovo War when her presence there could do no military good at all? Is it because Mr Campbell thought her presence would look good on TV?

Why did Britain publicly shy away from the idea of a ground invasion in that war when this actually emboldened Serbia? Because casualties would have damaged Labour in the polls.

Why does the Education Department produce almost nothing but stunts and gimmicks while it quietly goes about wrecking opt-out and grammar schools? Because the focus groups identified education as a big issue but Labour has no policy to improve it.

Why have millions been wasted on the "New Deal", which has found jobs for people who would almost certainly have found them anyway? Again, because its main purpose was propaganda.

Why was the Ulster peace process tested almost to destruction in mid-summer? Because Mr Blair wanted a spectacular triumph and probably because he hoped to devolve all three new toy parliaments – Wales, Scotland and Ulster – on the same day.

This Government has spent more of your money on advertising and upon press advisers and publicity operations than any British government in history. It is shameless about this horrible unfair abuse of its power – so shameless that it has now produced a sloppy worthless "annual report" on its doings, at taxpayers' expense, and had the nerve to try to sell it back to us, who paid for it.

This week, the Government's two main actions were attacks on the Opposition. The Prime Minister devoted a huge chunk of his poorly argued speech on Europe to an assault on the Tory Party.

The following day, the Home Secretary announced plans to make it almost impossible for the Tories to raise enough money to fight the next election.

The main concern of this Government, as Mr Blair has said in Parliament, is to destroy the Tories. This is because its real programme – the famous "Project" – cannot be sprung into action until after the next election. This must be won at all costs.

Soon after January's vast, ghastly, atheist celebration of Blairism at the Millennium Dome, temple of the Third Way, all this will reach its climax in a grossly unfair and dishonest election campaign, and the extinction of Britain as we have known it can proceed.

All the things Labour is coy about now – abolishing the pound, abolishing the traditional way of electing MPs, carving up England into Euro-regions, imposing punitive taxes on independent schooling, the end of marriage as a significant force, press laws, the final sell-out of Ulster – can then take place. As for taxes, well, they will be "harmonised" with those of our neighbours – and if you think that means they'll be reduced, poor old you.

Preparations for this, devolution, the neutering of the Lords and all the other things people mistakenly think are so dull, are being made now. But who cares? We are all much more worried about whether the Minister for Sport is an Arsenal or a Chelsea fan.

2/8/99

Sooner or later the Prime Minister is going to make himself burst into tears with his own oratory. Yesterday was a close-run thing.

As he began to emote about children playing safely in the nation's parks and every school being a good school, it was almost Kleenex time. Was he going to start babbling about lambs skipping in meadows? Perhaps next year.

This was, as it always is, a truly terrible speech. It had no poetry, no sense of history, no power to stir, no logic, no memorable phrase. Those who had read yesterday's papers had already seen most of it in the form of leaks.

The thing was a vast mountain range of humbug, so I only have room to graze lightly on its southern slopes. Let me suggest an alternative reading of one or two segments: "I know family life has changed", means Mr Blair is not prepared to defend marriage, without which there can be no family,

"Hot Spot policing", means highly-publicised periods of frantic police activity while the cameras watch, and then a return to normal. Proper intense policing needs to be backed by proper punishment, which is expensive and which Mr Blair does not believe in.

The promises he means to keep are mostly about spending your own money on our new nationalised industries – Frank Dobson's National Hypochondria Service and David Blunkett's National Ignorance Service. Money by itself does nothing for schools or hospitals, but it does ensure the jobs of public-service union members and helps to increase their pay.

Then there were the two passages which actually awoke enthusiasm in the hall. The first was praise for Marjorie Mowlam, who arranged our surrender to the IRA. The second was the promise to destroy the hereditary peerage – the last, narrow moat which protects the monarchy from Labour's closet republicans.

But if you wanted to weep at all, you might have done so when Mr Blair declared himself a patriot who wanted a strong United Kingdom. If this is what he does when he is feeling patriotic, what will he do when the mood passes?

30/9/98

BLAIRS

Kathy Gyngell, wife of the TV mogul Bruce, is urging Cherie Blair to do something really radical – look after her own children.

Even after freezing his pay, husband Tony can surely afford the loss of family income now that he has the Downing Street flat and Chequers.

After all, he seems to get his holidays almost free and doesn't need to worry about school fees, parking, commuting or telephone bills.

Writing in *Full Time Mothers*, a magazine that campaigns for just that, Mrs Gyngell says: "Tony Blair's agenda as Prime Minister can only mean that he is not available for his children.

"He is either travelling abroad, giving speeches, rushing back into Parliament or working through his red boxes in the wee small hours.

"His daughter Kathryn can hardly come bursting into a cabinet meeting to tell him of her woes, or get him to settle a fight with one of her elder brothers.

"Wouldn't he feel so much better then, if he could at least be sure that they had Mum to hand?"

She says that if Cherie had become PM, the new Ministry of Women could hardly have waited for Tony to don an apron and start wiping jam off the kitchen table.

"But could this have been asked of Cherie?" she adds. "Oh no! Her career must not be affected. What a fine example of modern womanhood!"

Mrs Gyngell argues that Cherie, with her name and reputation, hardly needs to worry about re-entering her profession as a barrister.

"What a wonderful precedent it would have set for all those women who dare not take time out for their families for fear they will jeopardise their careers for ever," she adds.

"Cherie Blair might be the icon of the women's movement, but to me her decision is an example of the selfishness that feminism encourages and makes acceptable."

Kathy Gyngell may say that. As a man, I couldn't comment.
22/9/97

Is the poor Queen ever again going to be safe from Tony Blair turning up wherever she goes, grinning wildly, making speeches, shaking hands with her subjects and generally trying to act as if he is her manager?

Perhaps she should create a special post for the Prime Minister, Brass Neck in Waiting or Silver Microphone of the Bedchamber, so that he can be guaranteed a choice spot and a speech at every royal occasion, from funerals to birthdays, christenings, weddings, divorces and visits to the dentist.

I have still not worked out what Mr Blair was doing at the monarch's Golden Wedding celebrations, leading her into lunch and making a speech of sticky banality, far outclassed by her own witty and literate one.

"The very best of British" indeed. It made Her Majesty sound like a pint of beer, a Yorkshire pudding or an Olympic bronze medal. Mr Blair is a politician, a party leader. He wants us to love him but, under our system, we do not have to do so if we do not want to do so (and millions do not want to, believe me).

What's more, Mr Blair does not seem to hold very strongly to the things the nation celebrated on Thursday – marriage and majesty.

Rather a lot of his chosen inner circle are unmarried by choice, or are homosexuals, or have divorced messily since they began working for him.

And until his clever aide Alastair Campbell spotted that the "People's Princess" might bring in some votes, Mr Blair thought that the monarchy was a meaningless cypher.

As for his claim that "modernity and tradition can live happily together", this just might be true. But tradition and majesty cannot survive Labour's urge to sweep away the old and tried.

Or why is the Royal Yacht *Britannia* being paid off for ever? 24/11/97

Cherie's over-exposed

I'm not obsessed with Cherie Booth, it's just that this supposedly non-political person can't seem to keep out of the papers.

The Premier's wife complained this week that the children of the poor can't become like her. True, but this is only because Labour schools policy has made it impossible to get a good education any more unless your parents are well-off or influential.

And you can hardly become a QC if you can't read. Mind you, you can hire Ms Booth to sue the school for you, as Pamela Phelps did last week, and then at least you'll be able to get a decent schooling for your children with your legal winnings.

Oh, and if Cherie really does not want to be associated with the cases she takes up, then she has no need whatsoever to be photographed next to her smiling client.

In fact, I can't recall another occasion when she has done this. 29/9/97

The Prime Minister seems to believe that his time is worth almost £7,000 an hour paid for by you and me. The seven hours he saved by going to and from America on Concorde instead of the usual plane – a slower and less showy RAF VC10 – cost an extra £47,962.

This will be raised by Hector the Inspector docking the

wages of school-dinner ladies, postmen, milkmen, teachers, nurses, car-workers and millions of others who can never hope to go by Concorde in their entire lives.

So what is the justification? Flying west across the Atlantic, and against the clock, there is no need to rush. You gain five hours in an ordinary plane. Mr Blair's big reason for hurrying back was not public business but a party speech, yesterday morning, to a Labour local government conference.

More important, his dash to Washington seems to have had no other purpose than rescuing Bill Clinton from disgrace. Nothing else happened that couldn't have been dealt with by our first-rate ambassador, Sir Christopher Meyer.

The Government will pretend that all this had a serious justification, that Saddam Hussein will be frightened by a show of solidarity and America will be grateful.

I don't think so. Saddam doesn't care and most of America still doesn't know that the melancholy remnants of the Royal Navy and the RAF have been sent out to hang around the edges of the US fleet in the Gulf.

The true act of solidarity was the Premier's presence at the side of the President, trying to reinforce him as he faced mockery and exposure for his reckless and trivial ways. Mr Blair certainly owes President Pantsdown a lot. Labour's tricksy election campaign, a triumph of the black arts over truth, was borrowed free of charge from Mr Clinton and his cynical honchos.

Gratitude is a decent emotion and, if Mr Blair wants to squander his undoubted personal integrity on bailing out a pal whose balance in the character bank is seriously overdrawn, it is rather touching.

I just don't see why we should have paid for it at all, let alone stumped up the extra so that he could ride to the rescue at twice the speed of sound.

I tried to obtain details of the use of Concorde by Tory Premiers. Downing Street said it was too difficult to find them out.

I wonder whether it will stick to this position if the Opposition takes the matter up.

9/2/98

Cherie Blair is getting above her station

I tried to hire the Royal Train yesterday. I thought that if Cherie Blair, a private citizen, could borrow it for a jaunt with a lot of other private citizens, that I would like to do so too.

It turns out that I am too private. When I called EWS, the company which now runs the train, it was unsympathetic to my plan.

"We are sure the use would not extend that far," it insisted. But what neither it nor any government department would say, because it is true but cannot yet be admitted, is that Cherie Blair's trip last Saturday marks a significant change in the British constitution.

More important, it is an open and official recognition that Britain now has a "First Lady" on the American pattern, who holds her position by virtue of being the Premier's wife.

So while this Government wants to stop people inheriting seats in the House of Lords, it is happy for people to obtain public office simply by being married to a member of the Government.

It is also a potent shift of majesty and reverence, from the throne to the elected Government, a halfway point between our fast-shrivelling monarchy and the Presidency which most Labour activists would like to see.

Socialists and radicals do not object to grandeur, pomp and luxury as such. Few in history have lived in such splendour, with so many servants, houses, private beaches, country estates, special trains, planes, hospitals and schools for their children, as did the elite of communist Russia.

But they do loathe to see these things in the hands of

conservative and traditional monarchy. Their complaints about the cost of the throne are really complaints about the continued existence of royalty. The Royal Train, which is hardly a fast or efficient way of getting about, especially from Birmingham to Chequers, was one of many symbols of the love and respect which British people felt for their monarchy.

They loved it because it represented them, their deepest feelings about their country, and also because it was above the trade of politics. But now we have a Prime Minister who is envious of that love and wants it for himself – the "pretty straight kinda guy" who deserves to be popular because he is so nice.

And now that Cherie has got away with borrowing the Royal Train, he can use it too.

One word of warning. Don't call it the "People's Train", because citizens may get the idea that their political masters' love of pomp has something to do with democracy, when it is really just a transfer of privilege from an old elite to a new one.

The rest of us people will just have to book seats on the Orient Express, if we can afford it.

21/5/98

Who cares what Tony Blair thinks about Frank Sinatra's death? Even if I had any affection for the violent, foul-mouthed, old mafioso, I wouldn't need the Prime Minister to feel my pain for me.

There is something very odd about Mr Blair's statement on this subject, odder even than his hijack of Princess Diana's flag-draped coffin and his weird emoting over Linda McCartney.

I can't believe pious Tony would have got on with Frank, whose crowd summed up their creed with the words: "You're not really drunk if you can lie on the floor without holding on." And *My Way*, that ghastly hymn to self love, is very different from the misty-eyed Third Way which Our Leader is treading in lonely splendour. "I have never met him or seen him perform," said the Premier. "But I have seen many of his films and heard his songs. I have grown up with Frank Sinatra and he will be deeply missed." So what? Why is it that every emotion has to be funnelled through, or expressed by, our Dear Leader Tony Blair? We elected him to run the country, not to offer us counselling or tell us when to cry.

Like so much of what this Government is doing, this has a creepy, totalitarian feel to it. Mr Blair says his party is the political arm of the whole British people, an astonishing claim not borne out by his capture of just 43.2 per cent of the votes in an election with the lowest turnout since the war.

Yet he acts as if he is the father of the nation, carried to power on the shoulders of millions, mainly because he is so personally wonderful that he is always right – "a pretty straight guy" of whom it is impossible to think any evil.

His alien Leaderism lies behind his bullying of the Queen, his scorn for Parliament and his hurried referendums in which the questions always put the opposition in the wrong before the campaign even begins.

It also helps to explain the disgraceful faked rally in Downing Street on the day after the election. Though this was entirely made up of Labour supporters with special passes, it has now become the standard photo-image of that startling day, suggesting falsely that Mr Blair was greeted by an ecstatic populace.

The open-mouthed collapse of opposition, the seizure of key points by political commissars in the Government Information Service and the refusal to answer hard questions all suggest that we now have continental-style government by leader.

Why is this serious? Because our unwritten constitution's firm foundation was the tradition of fairness, the idea that your opponent was not your enemy and that the government belonged to the Queen, not the other way round.

On this frail trust hang the independence of the courts, the neutrality of civil servants, the freedom of speech and thought. It is frighteningly easy to break – and I believe it is being broken now.

18/5/98

Ban hard core fawn

In a gutless age, let us strike a medal for Andrew Mackinlay, the Labour MP who refused to grovel to the People's Tony.

Mr Mackinlay asked the Prime Minister to condemn and reject the fawning tongue-on-toe-cap style of "questions" which he now faces from the robots and toadies who crowd the Government benches.

Well done, even if he may not specially want praise from me, and even if we probably wouldn't agree on anything else.

But the disturbing thing about this incident was that Our Leader did *not* seize the proffered chance to change the political climate.

Mr Blair should have said that while he did not enjoy being tripped up, teased, criticised and sometimes embarrassed, he recognised that this was the price of freedom, and so worth paying.

Instead, he dropped a rather heavy hint that Mr Mackinlay had blighted his chance of office.

There is no democratic spirit in this Government. Its instincts and reflexes are those of a dictatorship which is what it is in danger of becoming if it is not soon curbed.

4/6/98

Please pay more attention in future

I enjoy saying "I told you so" – one of the many underrated pleasures of being a pessimist.

During the last election, as some will recall, I had a little spat with the Great Leader of the People, as he then wasn't. He petulantly told me to stop being "bad" and to sit down, and threatened I would not be allowed to question him again.

All this palaver got in the way of the subject, which was his party's plan to wreck grant-maintained church schools, such as

171

the excellent London Oratory, by robbing them of the right to select their pupils.

The problem with this was that Mr Blair's two sons attend this school having been (quite rightly and fairly) selected. And Mr Blair had said in his manifesto in May 1997: "What I want for my own children, I want for yours."

But under his plans, cunningly concealed in that same manifesto, your children were going to get something very different from the young Blairs.

Hardly anyone was interested. The affair fizzled away to nothing. Now Labour has, as it said it would, pulled up the ladder behind Tony Blair.

In future, the school's crucial interview will only be able to ask about the family's religion and local Catholic children will get priority over those from distant addresses, such as Downing Street.

In a few years, about the time the Blairs leave, the special atmosphere and character of the London Oratory will change.

I suspect that its exam performance will drop and its discipline problems will increase as it becomes more like the other comprehensive schools which Labour love so much.

Did people vote for this? Did they think that "Education, education, education" meant the undermining of good schools? Perhaps not. But they will find over the next few years that the Labour manifesto is a document they should read very carefully indeed.

You could start a weasel farm with the number of weasel words and phrases in it.

But it's too late now. And I told you so. That'll teach you for not paying attention.

22/6/98

Come on, Tony, you can afford to pay for your own holidays now. You've got two free houses provided by the rest of us, a chauffeur-driven car, a high-earning wife and no school fees to worry about. So why do you have to take over an Italian prince's 50-room castle, just so you can avoid paying rent on a Tuscan villa of your very own?

Personally, I think that too long spent living off the State has sapped the Prime Minister's independence.

27/7/98

I hope for the sake of the country that Tony Blair's manager, scriptwriter and mental valet, Alastair Campbell, returns from holiday soon. Alastair seems to be the only person who knows where the widget is which connects Mr Blair's brain with his mouth.

Our Prime Minister said last week that he was "totally determined to wage war against terrorism in all its forms". He said this in part payment of his huge debt to Bill Clinton, who lent him the slick, dishonest election campaign that got him in to Downing Street.

But, as they say in the USA: like, HELLO? Mr Blair has just agreed to release a whole prison full of terrorists. There are no plans to rain cruise missiles down on certain addresses in West Belfast, County Armagh and Dundalk, where some forms of terrorism are plotted. Next time, Tony, at least leave out the "in all its forms" part.

24/8/98

Is Sloaney Tony the new Diana?

I warned you last week that Holy Tony would start appearing in hospital wards, and it now seems he is turning into the new Princess Diana, haunting midnight scenes of suffering and woe with a beatific smile on his face.

The poor fellow has to have something to do while Alastair Campbell runs the country. I revealed many months ago that

Alastair, officially Blair's press secretary and mental valet, was the real power in the Government. This has now been confirmed by Lord Cranborne, who says the Prime Minister told him he would have to check the details of an agreement with Alastair before putting it into effect.

Anyone who has met both men knows that Alastair has the brains, wit and force of personality of a natural leader, while Tony has the rather dim sweetness of an ambitious but not very clued-up Sloane Ranger.

The problem is that rough, tough Alastair would terrify the trousers off the voters if he were ever let near a microphone or allowed to be interviewed. So Tony gets the title, the house and the car.

18/1/99

How can anyone possibly be as perfect as Tony?

A cross reader telephoned me last week to complain that I had referred to the Prime Minister as Princess Tony. Let me explain: the Dear Leader *is* worryingly like the late People's Princess. Not only does he have the same air of a tall, rather dim Sloane Ranger on the make, he also manages to behave extremely badly without damaging his popularity.

It's always someone else's fault when anything goes wrong. Aides and colleagues crash in flames but his role is never questioned. Attempts to interview him always run up against his own conviction that he is so good, kind and wonderful that it is actually rather wicked to doubt his perfection.

He loves stealing the limelight from the real Royal Family and obviously thoroughly enjoys the palaces, banquets, limousines and VIP lounges of life.

And then there are the photo-opportunities, preferably among children, the cynical manipulator's favourite backdrop because the mere presence of the young deflects criticism and suggests a deep and sincere concern for the next generation.

It had been worrying me for months. I had also been unconvinced by all the other candidates for the post of the "New Diana", none of whom had quite the same weird appeal. But when he conducted an imaginary rescue of a man who hadn't been drowning and began to appear in hospitals, it all fell into place. Only one thing baffles me. While Princess Tony obviously isn't running the country – a task he leaves to his mental valet Alastair Campbell – where *does* he find time to write so many newspaper articles? He was scribbling in my local evening paper last week. It is an astonishing achievement, even for a People's Princess.

1/2/99

Princess Tony was asked in Parliament last Wednesday if he saw any role for marriage in his family policy. I have held his answer up to the light, tried it in the mirror and bombarded it with electrons. It appears to be "no", despite his enormous efforts to present himself as a traditional family man. One thing I have noticed about this Prime Minister is that the more he *appears* to support something – be it the United Kingdom, the middle class, the monarchy, low taxation or good schools – the more danger that something is in.

8/2/99

Where does Tony find the time?

I continue to be amazed at Princess Tony's career as a journalist. His articles, on dozens of subjects, appear everywhere. You would have thought he would be proud of this and perhaps keep (as I still do) a book of cuttings.

As G. K. Chesterton wrote rather sentimentally when he was fat and rich: "I dream of the days when work was scrappy, and rare in our pockets the mark of the mint, when we were angry and poor and happy and proud of seeing our names in print."

Perhaps the Princess doesn't care. Anyway, Downing Street claims there is no record of his output since May 1997. Sadly nobody else has kept his scribblings either, so far as I know, so I can't tell you how many thousands of words he has written per month, while not busy abolishing the country.

There are people who collect beer mats, cricket balls, menus and seed catalogues. Is there some lone eccentric out there with an attic full of the works of Tony who can help me?

8/3/99

For safety's sake, open a 'Tony Only' lane

I think we should have a special Princess Tony lane on all our motorways, and also down the middle of the main streets of our major cities. Otherwise, the Princess is going to have to stay at home all the time.

You see, it's now official that it's too dangerous for him to be stuck in a traffic jam. Somewhere among the motionless motor cars there could be an assassin waiting anywhere. Despite being so popular, the Princess apparently has many deadly enemies.

So when his armour-plated Jaguar swung into the empty bus lane on the M4 motorway, sweeping regally past thousands of immobilised voters, it was on security grounds.

Put out of your mind any thought that it was because our petulant, short-tempered leader was cross at having to wait in traffic like an ordinary citizen.

In fact, according to the officially-leaked version of events, it wasn't his decision at all. His Special Branch bodyguards decided it was a security risk to leave him trapped in the jam. And – what a coincidence – they are allowed to break highway regulations if they think he has been left open to attack.

Did the most popular man in Britain protest fiercely at his bodyguards' decision? Did he have to be overruled by them before allowing himelf to be driven down the bus lane?

Or did he perhaps have serious second thoughts only *after* he decided to jump the queue. Then – too late – did he see the faces of the people he had bypassed and realise they could recognise him and would remember?

Special lanes for the socialist elite used to exist – in Moscow. One, electrically heated to stop it icing up in winter, ran right past my block of flats. The excuse for that was security, too.

28/6/99

BBC

The BBC has broken its promise and is failing in its duty

When is the BBC going to regain its manhood? Since May 1, it seems to have had a rather painful operation, which has made it incapable of criticising or standing up to the Government.

During the long years of the Tories, BBC Radio and TV interviewers piled into ministers with gusto, often leaving them gasping. John Humphrys and Jeremy Paxman became famous for their refusal to take waffle for an answer.

Criticised for being anti-Tory, the BBC quite reasonably explained that it was its duty to behave like this. The actual opposition, the Labour Party, was in a hospital for the politically insane for most of the period, and couldn't do the job.

And it promised that, if Labour ever came to power, it would be just as tough. That promise has been broken, and broken and broken. The BBC, which is paid for by a poll-tax levied on all of us, is failing in its clear duty.

When did you last hear, or see, a truly aggressive interview with a minister? How often do Opposition spokesmen get the chance to rebut the propaganda put out by the Government's ever-active briefing teams? How often do Labour's dissidents get an opportunity to air their differences with St Tony of the Internet?

How often does the BBC stand up – and I mean really stand up – to the bullying and manipulation it suffers? Isn't it about time it revealed how the Government kills discussion by threatening to withdraw ministers from programmes? This is a very effective way of blackmailing producers into banning awkward customers from the airwaves.

Why doesn't it call the bullies' bluff and run the programmes anyway, with an empty chair – or a tub of lard – labelled with the absent minister's name? If they refuse to come, they can hardly complain they've been unfairly treated.

I was the first to notice the nasty, undemocratic tendency of the Blair regime, something others are beginning to spot.

The attempt to turn the neutral government information service into a propaganda department, the sidelining of Parliament, the dislike of proper questioning, the way new MPs were ordered to think as they were told, were all bad enough.

Now we learn of a plan to use taxpayers' money to set up a media monitoring unit to keep an eye on comments in the Press. Surely ministers can read the papers themselves? There is something fishy and un-British about a Government which monitors people's opinions.

Our new masters need a good shaking. The BBC has the power and the skills to provide it. Or has it decided that its initials actually stand for Blair's Broadcasting Castration?
20/10/97

Congratulations to 12-year-old Oliver Tickner for catching the BBC's cultural revolutionaries red-handed. Oliver was watching a teatime children's show called *Pirates* and discovered it was packed with anti-Tory propaganda.

If he hadn't complained, they would have got away with it, as they do in almost every area of broadcasting, including alleged comedy.

What sort of person, you might wonder, thinks he or she is entitled to bend the minds of children with partisan bias?

Has anyone actually been reprimanded for this?
10/11/97

I have in front of me the BBC producers' guidelines, a fascinating document which seeks to instruct the programme makers of that great corporation.

On page 74, it warns against "inaccurate or hurtful stereotypes".

"BBC programmes should not categorise black people as criminals, women as housewives, disabled people as victims, gay people as ineffectual, old people as incapable."

Say that again slowly. As far as the BBC are concerned, being a housewife is the equivalent of being a criminal, a victim, ineffectual or incapable.

This shows dangerous contempt for the brave, determined women who defy fashion and economic pressure and stay at home to raise their own children. I urge the BBC to stop stereotyping homemakers and full-time mothers.

3/11/97

And from No. 10 . . .

Have you noticed that more and more TV news reports on politics are delivered from outside No. 10 Downing Street, when they used to be done with Parliament in the background?

Is anyone encouraging the idea that we now have a sort of president, or did it just happen?

Also, if you watch these reports carefully, this is what you will see. First, a brief summary of the story. Second, an interview with a Government person giving their point of view. Third, an interview with an Opposition person giving their point of view. Fourth, a summing-up by the correspondent retailing the Government Press Officer line, and so wrapping up the item with a pro-Labour tinge.

Excuse me, but this is not actually balanced.

6/4/98

Labour look vacant

Congratulations to BBC's *Newsnight* programme. A few weeks ago, I suggested that they should display an empty chair whenever Labour refused to take part in a debate. On Thursday night they did just that, to great effect. I shall try to take credit for this. Then, on Friday night, interviewer Jeremy Paxman subjected Propaganda Minister Peter Mandelson to the sort of interrogation he used to hand out to the Tories. Punches were landed.

Sadly, Mr Mandelson was in a remote studio (I wonder why?), which made it easier for him to evade the questions.

But it was a good night for democracy and fairness, and a hopeful sign that the BBC may at last be recovering its missing manhood.

17/11/97

Sauce for the goose?

The People's Commissariat for Bullying and Censorship, alias the Labour Party Press Office, has decided to lean on John Humphrys and the BBC's *Today* programme.

Mr Humphrys is supposed to have been unkind to the Secretary of State for Compulsory Wageslave Motherhood, Harriet Harman. He is said to have cruelly interrupted her and persisted with questions when she failed to answer them.

Poor John hasn't yet understood that the BBC is only supposed to do this to the Tories.

His colleague, Sue MacGregor, on the other hand, seems to have grasped this perfectly. On Saturday morning, she railed at poor Michael Howard for refusing to praise the Prime Minister's great achievement, ie being flattened by the European Union.

Didn't the BBC used to say something about how it was its job to subject the Government to proper questioning? By the way, I am still waiting for a number of promised written replies to complaints about BBC bias in favour of the single currency. Have any of you had the same experience?

15/12/97

I am quite sure Lance Price carried out his job as a BBC political reporter with commendable impartiality. And I congratulate him upon his appointment as a special adviser to the Prime Minister.

However, I do not congratulate the BBC for its attitude, or non-attitude, towards this event. If current BBC political reporters think that they are in line for government jobs, isn't it just a teeny weeny bit possible that it may influence their attitude towards ministers, even though it obviously didn't influence Mr Price?

Yet the BBC has no plans to change its rules to cope with this possibility. Perhaps it might reconsider. Can you imagine what would have happened if a BBC political staffer had gone to work for Margaret Thatcher as a political appointee?

22/6/98

It is time we reformed some of the most powerful and least democratic areas of British politics – the posts of Lord High Inquisitioner at the BBC, currently held by a select and privileged group of men and women.

These few immensely powerful people are unelected. Picked by a mysterious magic circle whose identities and politics are a secret to the public. Yet they are paid for by a hefty poll tax, known misleadingly as a "TV licence" but levied on every home in the land under pain of imprisonment. Unlike the other poll tax, payment is not even rewarded with a vote.

Currently, the senior Lord High Inquisitioner is Mr Jeremy

Paxman, who is charming and delightful in private but is required to wear a bullying manner in public, much as the Lord Chancellor used to be made to wear tights and buckled shoes.

Last week, the unelected Mr Paxman entered the row about the powers of the House of Lords. In his courtroom, sorry studio, were two Tories, Lord Hunt and Liam Fox MP, and one Labour minister, Lord Williams of Mostyn.

The Tories, despite being the Opposition, were the first to undergo Mr Paxman's brand of tough questioning. Not very interested in the issue of closed lists – in which party officials rather than voters pick Euro-MPs – he chastised them for frustrating the will of the Government.

He opened his interrogation of Lord Hunt with the words: "You used to be an honest man." And then, after the two Tories had defended themselves as best they could, he turned to the Government Minister and *invited him to take over the questioning*.

The undemocratic nature of the Lords was explored in depth but the undemocratic nature of the closed list system was hardly considered. And at two points he actually laughed at the minister's rather feeble jokes.

As I have said before here, I rather like Mr Paxman and his combative style. I think it is a good thing that governments are given a hard pounding and I think the Tories must learn to look after themselves with a bit more guts and spirit.

But I think the BBC must understand a couple of things. It is because this country has a free opposition that it is a free country.

Attacking the Opposition, simply for being the Opposition, is dangerous to democracy. There are plenty of newspaper journalists only too willing to suck up to Downing Street these days, without the BBC joining in.

The Tories have now been out of power for more than 18 months.

Habits of mind formed during nearly two decades of Tory government are obviously hard to break but, if the BBC does not soon discover that Labour is now the Government and needs to be harried night and morning, then people will begin to wonder why they should be obliged to pay for it.

23/11/98

So now what will the BBC be calling itself?

The BBC no longer wants to talk about "Britain" or the "British". I am not surprised but I don't really blame the Corporation, even though many of its staff seem not to like this country. Increasingly, it has no choice. People are starting to realise that Britain, as we knew and loved it, has now been abolished by Princess Tony.

We are like the man in the cartoon who sits complacently in his armchair while a villain on the floor below saws away the planks beneath his feet. By the time we have realised what is going on, we are already plunging through the hole. For years, the education industry and our cultural elite have undermined and denigrated Britain, nibbling and hacking away at its institutions, from the family and the grammar schools to Parliament and the monarchy.

They cleared the way for the swift, unfair referendums which last year broke up the UK. They hope they have prepared the ground for the final death blow to Britain, the abolition of the pound.

We are living in the midst of a silent but devastating revolution which will end in tears.

5/4/99

I continue to be quite overwhelmed by your many e-mails and letters, from readers of all ages, about the poison and slime which comes out of our TV sets.

I was much encouraged by the story of one young family which had exiled the TV set and rediscovered civilised life.

But what can we do about the cultural dictators who insist on forcing *their* tastes and *their* politics on us. In the case of the BBC, which last week lost all objectivity in its coverage of the launch of the euro-rouble, we have a powerful weapon.

Just as the American colonists began their revolution with the cry "No taxation without representation", TV licence payers have the right to insist that their views are taken into account in future.

I like the BBC, and think our broadcasting would be a lot worse without it, but I think that viewers are entitled to a number of things:

• Mainstream entertainment should not set out to push the boundaries of language and taste.

• Older and sweeter forms of drama and comedy should no longer be treated with bitter, snobbish contempt.

• Minority tastes can and should still be catered for, but not favoured over everything else.

The corporation's many fine reporters and presenters are overwhelmingly people of the Left, who seldom even try to conceal this nowadays.

It is time they were balanced by others from the Right who are now all but excluded from such jobs by an unspoken but powerful convention.

The BBC should remember that it is paid for by people of all tastes and political views, not just London professional liberals who let their children swear.

11/1/99

Battling for the truth

The BBC now takes the view that the opinions of its elite are "normal" and that everything outside its narrow, socialist liberalism is "extreme". This leads to the demented idea that the wild experiment of abolishing the pound is mainstream thinking, when overwhelming millions oppose it.

For some time, I have urged the Corporation to try a different approach and allow its presenters to reveal their true feelings so that we could have a proper national debate. No dice.

In a small way, I am now trying to show them that a different method might get to the truth more reliably. Each Sunday morning, on Talk Radio, Labour's Derek Draper and I examine the issues of the week from Left and Right.

No one gets away with anything but nor are valid views brushed aside or suppressed.

21/12/98

Why I'm glad to see Greg running the Beeb

I am delighted that Greg Dyke is the new boss of the BBC. Thanks to his appointment, the total and shameless Left-wing bias of the Corporation is now on public view, undeniable and blatant. In which case, something may be done about this huge and growing scandal.

In fact Mr Dyke − who has a sense of humour and an instinct for fairness − is far better placed to clean up this mess than a Tory or a supposedly neutral bureaucrat. By the way, why did Maggie Thatcher appoint John Birt, a closet Labour supporter, to the same job?

Mr Dyke and I were at York University at the same time. He was a mature student and I was an immature student. I was rather touched that in those days of Left-wing passion he clung, unfashionably, to the Labour Party he loves. In all the wretched years between, he has never wavered. I really hope he can be persuaded not to resign from it now, after so many decades of loyalty.

It would be a pointless action, as well as a sad one. You may hand in a party card but you cannot resign from your instincts or your friendships and you should not be expected to do so.

Anyway, it is not a man's open political links that lead to bias. If your slant is known to all, you cannot secretly influence others. The bias of the BBC is not crudely party political, though it certainly does not like the Tory Party.

It is felt on a hundred issues, from marriage to Europe, from the Middle East to homosexuality. It appears in soap operas as well as on the news. It is often unconscious. The BBC simply assumes that its soppy liberal view of the world is "the consensus" – ie right, while the rest of us are "extreme", ie wrong.

Keep your Labour Party card, Greg, but sort out the intolerant conformists who are wrecking a great national institution.

28/6/99

HUMAN RIGHTS

A criminal annoyed with his soggy cornflakes? Queue here

Do you feel any more free than you did last week, now that Tony Blair has decided to "protect" your human rights? I certainly don't. I have suspected since this Government came to power that it was a threat to liberty of speech and thought, and my suspicions grow each week.

Let us look at these alleged "rights" that are now going to be enforced by the courts, with the power to compel Parliament to change the law in a matter of days. Will they increase freedom or undermine it?

Queue here if you are a homosexual soldier who thinks his pleasure is more important than the national defence, or a convicted criminal who is annoyed that his cornflakes are too soggy. Step this way if you are a paedophile who wants his identity protected, or a politician who wants to hide behind a screen of "privacy".

Get your application in if you are the relative of an IRA bomber who has walked into a British Army bullet, or a schoolteacher who wants to tell her pupils where they can get the contraceptive pill for free.

This is no more than a giant Whingers' Charter, designed to enforce and extend every modish prejudice of the conformist Left.

And it is a deep insult to the truly free people of this country, who have always known that liberty depends upon self-restraint, duty and obligation, not on scores of selfish demands for special treatment.

Labour's private attitude toward freedom is revealed by their persecution of the party's own Euro-MPs, who have been told to shut up, or be ground into the dust. Anyone with a free bone in his body must *instinctively* find this disturbing.

I know these Euro-MPs are unattractive, with unpleasant views. But this is exactly why they have been chosen as the first victims, and why true lovers of freedom have to support them.

If they are squashed, Westminster MPs will be next, and then . . .

Mr Blair has become very used to getting his own way inside his rather miserable party, and even in his circle of admirers.

I am told that those close to his throne, like to swear and shout a lot at underlings.

I am also told that impatience, petulance and a humourless, thin-skinned refusal to take criticism are common among his courtiers, along with vindictiveness.

The saint-like Tony, of course, is immune from these vices. But he should recognise that such coarse manners are much more common in dictatorships than they are in democracies.

27/10/97

Time the rest of us won back our rights

For millions of us, the once noble words "human rights" mean foreign interference, busybodies and pettifogging inquests into perfectly sensible trials. What has happened to our world, that an idea which sounds so bright and shining should now produce weary shrugs and bitter jokes?

Yet that is the response of many to the European Human Rights Commission's condemnation of the trial of the two boys who killed James Bulger.

How long, we wonder, before some self-righteous tribunal of alleged experts comes up with a reason to release Myra Hindley, the Yorkshire Ripper, Dennis Nilsen and dozens more ghastly wrongdoers now locked away in the dark corners of the penal system?

And why is it that these precious "human rights" never seem to apply to the small businessman crushed by relentless demands from the taxman, to the householder who tries to defend his property against thieves when the police can't or won't help – in short, to the good little people who play by the rules and yet get caught in some hideous twist of bad luck?

Why is it that the people whose "rights" we are always being pressed to support so often turn out to be pressure groups with radical agendas, when they are not actually convicted criminals? The truth is that this ringing phrase is a phoney. In a truly free society, as this was until very recently, the citizen had no need of individual rights.

He is free to start with. If the government wishes to tell him what to do, it must get laws passed by a free parliament, or confirmed by independent courts. The only rights we ever needed were those won in 1688, when the power of the king was curbed for good.

It is the same in the USA, where the great Bill of Rights – modelled on ours – is not a list of things you can do but a list of things the government cannot do.

I have begun to notice that the more I hear about rights, the fewer I seem to have. I have seldom felt so hedged about with regulation, so that I am now even told what I can eat.

Nor am I happy about freedom of speech in a society where tens of thousands of students are being taught that certain thoughts are unthinkable, certain things unsayable. Last year, I was ordered off the platform at a student meeting for voicing what were judged to be unacceptable opinions about homosexuality and women's equality.

Perhaps I should have taken the case to the European Court of Human Rights. But would I have been treated with the same consideration as a killer who didn't like his sentence? I wonder.
22/3/99

SOFT ON COMMUNISM

True blue traitors?

Long-secret papers from the KGB reveal that the Kremlin recruited a band of Oxford agents before the war, around the time it was hiring Philby, Burgess and Maclean at Cambridge. The difference is that the Russians still refuse to identify the Oxford lot.

Their leader, codenamed Scott, urged Stalin to make full use of him and his fellow students: "We could, for example, get our people to be bishops, Army, Navy and Air Force top brass, highly placed civil servants, bankers, members of the Conservative Party and police chiefs."

Well, given what has happened to the country, the Church, the Tory Party, the Armed Forces and the police, I think we are entitled to wonder if the Oxford communists weren't a good deal more successful than their flashier Cambridge comrades.

19/1/98

Perhaps Pol Pot is dead, perhaps not. It does not really matter. Marxist idealism, the self-righteous false religion which led straight to the boneyards and concentration camps of Cambodia, Korea, China and Russia, is still very much alive, stronger than ever in spite of its repeated failures and disasters.

All it needs to flourish is a little war and instability, which are just over our horizon thanks to the planned single currency and NATO expansion. Perhaps, in one of our joke universities, a mild-mannered lecturer is even now at work, who will be Britain's Pol Pot.

20/4/98

I couldn't care less who manipulates the toadying press on behalf of Gordon Brown. In the midst of a slow-motion coup d'etat, with the independence of my country threatened, I have more important things on my mind.

But why does nobody seem to care that Charlie Whelan was a Communist Party member until 1990, 30 years after Stalin's horrors were revealed. What would have gone on if a Tory Cabinet minister's closest aide had once been in the British Union of Fascists?

11/1/99

At last, Gulag gives up its secrets

I implore you to set aside three hours of your life next Saturday evening to watch a television programme. It is called *Gulag* and goes out on BBC2. I recommend that you fortify yourself with plenty of vodka, black bread and strong Russian tea.

For the first time on British television, the monstrous scale of Soviet crimes against humanity will be properly related. Because Stalin's camps were never liberated and rot to this day in remote places where few will ever go, they have never burned themselves on to the world's conscience.

There is, of course, another reason. The largely left–liberal elite which runs the media does not like to admit that the USSR was even more murderous than the Third Reich – the death tally may have reached 50 million.

The programme draws you slowly into the inner circle of horror. It opens in a baking Russian summer among the deep, haunted forests near Moscow and, mile by mile, takes you into Siberia. It is worth seeing alone for the camera's heart-stopping aerial approach to the ghastly city of Norlisk, the very suburbs of Hell. As one who spent more than two years in the USSR, I wish that anything I had ever written could have conveyed so well the desolation of Soviet life.

One horror is piled on another, made all the more powerful by the individual memory of arrest, interrogation, the sudden end of happy life and the plunge into the whirlwind of despair and suffering: the tragic crowds of Lithuanian deportees defiantly singing a hymn to the Virgin Mary in tears as they are marched to the eastbound trains and a lone, brave priest blesses them; the woman who will never trust another human being till she dies, after being betrayed in the camps; the awful, self-serving secret policemen and guards and commandants who, to this day, yearn for the return of Comrade Stalin; the camp slave-driver who shoved living men into a collapsing dam to shore it up.

Watch for the majestic locks where the cruise-ships pass by, their passengers all unknowing that skeletons are concealed in the concrete; the man who escaped and whose parents tried in vain to warn the world that wasn't interested; the women with their wombs hanging down between their knees because of overwork, the awful pictures, drawn from the life of the camp world, which ought to be as well-known as the photographs of Belsen, but which cannot find a publisher.

This is no easy thing to watch. But once you have seen it you will begin to understand why the noble slogans of socialism, such talk as "for the many, not the few", the "people's this and the people's that" and "we are doing this for the children", "the future not the past" and "the hand of history" make my stomach heave.

If you think your goals are good, there is no limit to the evil you can do.
5/7/99

A batty 87-year-old woman says she gave our nuclear secrets to a vile and murderous tyranny, apparently because Joe Stalin kept the Moscow trolleybus fares down. I say, leave her to die in peace because I believe in mercy and pity. But if she'd spied for Stalin's twin, Hitler, I bet she'd be in Holloway already, having her fingerprints taken. Why is that?
13/9/99

MISCELLANEOUS

Imprisoned by a ring of steel

You must have noticed the rather aggressive, spiked steel fences that are springing up everywhere, especially round schools and along railway lines.

They are called "palisade" fencing and I rang up one of the firms which makes them. They said Britain is now building hundreds of miles of them each year. Originally, they were seen mainly in the North, where people are used to harsher landscapes, but they are now spreading to the South.

This is yet more evidence, that if people won't behave, they forge chains and build prison walls for themselves. If we don't rediscover right and wrong, I repeat my prediction that in 20 years' time, we will look back fondly on the days when we could still have glass windows in our houses.

27/10/97

Yes, yes, I know that smoking in aircraft lavatories can be dangerous. But people wouldn't do it if airlines hadn't all become anti-tobacco fanatics and abolished their smoking zones.

A reader e-mails me to tell a ludicrous but true story of anti-smoking zealotry. Desperate for solace on a long-haul flight, he was reduced to sucking on one of those plastic nicotine tubes. His neighbour angrily summoned a stewardess and denounced him, claiming she was afraid nicotine might leak into her airspace.

Passive non-smoking, I suppose.

3/8/99

Charlie's personal hang-up

I haven't had much to do with Mr Charles Whelan, the profane ex-communist who now runs Her Majesty's Treasury, with a little help from a glum-looking Scotsman called Gordon Brown.

This is because I once rang him up and asked him for a fact on the record. He began to issue forth a stream of "guidance", which I did not need. I politely told him that I just wanted the on-the-record fact.

He was so shocked that he slammed the phone down, and has pretended to be out whenever I have called since. I am rather proud of this and advise all other self-respecting journalists to get him to hang up on them, too.

Deprived of his spin-doctor, Mr Brown might then be forced to tell us the truth: that he longs to wreck the British economy by giving all his remaining powers to a bank in Germany, but that he is scared that the voters will think this is a stupid idea once they grasp what it means.

The government has the same problem with many other policies, especially education. It knows that what it wants to do will not be popular. So it employs public relations men to brief in whispers, and it is scared of Parliament, where everything is on the record.

27/10/97

Pressure on to cook the books

Fire chiefs are claiming that the water companies have turned down pressure in the mains, so as to cut the amount they lose in leaks without actually having to repair rusting pipes.

This is a result of regulation by politicians who haven't heard of the Law of Unintended Consequences.

What does this mean in practice? Passengers' Charter

penalties for late trains have slowed railways down. To avoid forking out, the companies have changed timetables so journeys often take longer than they did 15 years ago.

School league tables have led to dumbed-down exams and to heads preventing children from taking GCSEs and A-levels unless they are sure of getting good grades.

And the obsession with the rate of youth unemployment has led to the barmy expansion of the Universities, where tens of thousands of youngsters waste three years obtaining meaningless degrees – but are kept off the dole.

I am sure there are plenty of other examples of the way that, as soon as any statistic becomes important it gets massaged.
23/3/98

Christopher Howes disappeared two years ago in Cambodia where he was bravely clearing mines. His Khmer Rouge captors offered to let him go but he insisted on staying with his companion, a local interpreter who had been snatched with him. I am immensely moved by this act of courage and generosity.

Please remember Christopher and his family in your thoughts.
6/4/98

Why no law to ban this Suburban Sadist?

Only one member of my household hunts. I disapprove strongly of what he does. Perhaps I should find a Labour MP to get up a campaign against him.

What I most dislike is the way he seems to enjoy torturing the creatures he catches. Sometimes we manage to rescue his victims but usually they are horribly wounded and have to be killed. He is rather keen on murdering young animals and baby birds. He and millions like him are allowed to follow their cruel instincts, regardless of season and untroubled by hunt saboteurs. Yet he is always welcome in my home.

He is, of course, a cat; the bloody sadist of the suburbs and countryside, killing for sport alone – and who is to say his small furred and feathered victims feel any less pain than foxes or stags?

In their current spasms of useless sentimentality about foxes, do any of our anti-cruelty campaigners have any plans to control my cat and all the others? Do they show us blown-up pictures of his disembowelled and dismembered prey?

Of course they don't. Their whole effort is nothing to do with cruelty, which they accept in so many other areas. It is just a spiteful attack on a world they do not understand and so despise.

1/12/97

A soft spot for the prime-time porkers

Like the millions who have hoped that the two ginger Tamworths would make a clean getaway, I like pigs a lot.

This is mainly because I once took a summer job looking after them. They were friendly, intelligent and rather touchingly came to recognise that the approaching noise of my motorbike meant food was on its way. Then came the awful day when they had to be bundled into vans and sent off to the bacon factory. I could only watch, a white-faced townie, as the farmer and his sons flung my doomed squealing friends into a grubby van. I wanted to protest.

Yes of course it was the farmer who was right and I who was wrong. You never hear of pig's milk or cheese or pig wool. We wouldn't keep these creatures unless we were going to eat them.

But I agree it would be much more honest if we were just

allowed to eat animals that we had killed ourselves. There is something wrong with a world where we only ever see the animal kingdom sliced and packaged in supermarket chill trays.

19/1/98

Taste of real life

I learned more from my weeks working in a brewery than in many months of university. Starting at 7.30 each morning, I slung crates, rolled barrels and stretched my hamstrings amid the steam of the hellish bottle washing machine.

At the end of each day, I was so shattered that I was quite capable of watching the worst that the television industry could pump out. I counted every penny of the 11 pounds, 13 shillings and fourpence (£11.67) that I took home (this was 1969).

I was quite justly thumped by the foreman for being a pain in the neck and learned a lot of new and uncomplimentary expressions. For years, I have looked fondly at the place as I have gone by. There, I think I started to grow up. It also makes good beer and once a week blankets my home town with a lovely yeasty smell of brewing that is as English as a Turner painting.

This week, for business reasons which are quite beyond me, it faces closure. I am outraged and, if I were a millionaire, I would buy it and keep it open. Sadly I am not.

13/7/98

Brother of all battles

Some of you may have been a little puzzled last week to read in the pages of this newspaper about a certain Christopher Hitchens, who plans to attack the People's Princess in a Channel 4 TV programme. As you will find if you watch this, he sounds a bit like me (we can impersonate each other on the phone) and some claim we look alike, though we both deny it.

Are we related? Well, yes, Christopher is my big brother, and the Left-wing half of the family. Although I largely agree with him about the adulation of Diana, and we compete to see who can scorn Bill Clinton more, we quarrel on.

This has been going on for a long time. As I lay gurgling in my pram at the top of a steep hill, Christopher released the brakes. He was later disturbed while feeding me what he believed to be poisonous leaves.

In turn, he recalls sitting admiring a flowerbed (this seems unlikely to me, but he swears it's true) when he was alerted by a sinister shadow. Turning round, he was in time to see me, barely able to walk, staggering towards him with a rake in my hands and a wicked glint in my eye.

Our war continued for years, and our parents once compelled us to sign a peace treaty on Northern Irish lines, which I'm ashamed to say I quickly repudiated.

All that's over now and instead we just have civilised arguments about matters of principle. Amateur psychiatrists can get lost.

24/9/98

I was invited to the London party where Left-wing columnist Polly Toynbee chucked wine over Right-winger Bruce Anderson, and I am cross that nobody threw wine over me. There I was, entirely surrounded by leftist foes, telling them they were too stupid to understand that Tony Blair was the most extremist Prime Minister for decades, and they just listened politely. Maybe next time.

26/10/98

Time for these teen rebels to grow up

I am not particularly upset that the old monster Augusto Pinochet should have been woken at midnight and told he was under arrest. I do not think any cause can justify torture and murder of political opponents.

Chile's current prosperity does not excuse these evil acts and nor does General Pinochet's welcome help to this country during the Falklands War.

What I object to about the whole Pinochet business is that it is not the action of a serious country. A serious country would not have got involved in such a silly piece of political street theatre. It would have found a missing semi-colon in the extradition warrant and bundled the old generalissimo on to the first plane out. It would have seen the endless daft complications it now faces. It would have realised that this is Chile's business not ours.

But we have a Government whose senior members are, deep down, not yet grown-up. They have never really got over their student days when Left-wing socialism was the faith that they lived by.

Speaking as a former student Trotskyite rabble-rouser who had his share of brawls with the police and once (oh shame) chanted "Ho! Ho! Ho Chi Minh!" outside the US Embassy in Grosvenor Square, I can remember how much fun it was and how we longed for power so that we could revenge ourselves on the wicked Right-wing Establishment.

But the time comes when you get over it, when you understand that this sort of thinking is the mirror image of beliefs which persuaded General Pinochet that he was justified in his grisly slaughter and torture. At least, that is what I thought. But do not be fooled by those suits and those receding hairlines.

Our Cabinet is still in the grip of the dangerous teenage ideas that they held in their distant campus days, ideas tinged with intolerance and petty spite. They enjoy arresting their opponents in the middle of the night. Governments should not do that. It is time they grew out of it.

26/10/98

Driving damages us more

Health Secretary Frank Dobson began another assault on smoking this week. As a personal smoke-free zone, I serve no special interests here but I make two points.

The more authority attacks smoking, the more young people will do it. I don't smoke mainly because my parents and teachers did, making it hard for me to view it as glamorous or rebellious.

Second, why just smoking? Why not target driving? The moment you start driving a car, you begin to get fat, wheezy and unfit, a perfect target for heart disease. You also become more selfish and bad tempered, which smokers often aren't.

And you give off evil-smelling poisonous fumes which, in summer, form great brown domes of smog over our cities.

Given the choice, I'd rather put up with secondhand smoke than first-hand smog.

14/12/98

As I bicycled homewards up an ill-lit hill, an approaching car suddenly swerved. There was a nasty bang, the sort that fills you with dread. The car slowed and then sped away. On the road lay a small muntjak deer about the size of a dog, quite common in my part of the country, twitching and kicking piteously. I do not think I could have borne it if it had cried out as well.

I could neither kill the beast nor help it. I felt, with self-disgust, how useless we modern people are with our computer skills and our driving licences and our degrees. Thank heaven,

201

the poor thing died as I looked on. I was cross with myself for being no help and bitterly angry with the driver who could not even be bothered to stop and see what he had done. I bet he is against fox-hunting.

18/1/99

The East German secret police, I learn, once kept a store of the used socks of dissidents and troublemakers, in case it was ever necessary to hunt them down with bloodhounds and they needed their scent.

So now I know why I have so many single socks. MI5 has them filed for when I try to flee the Thought Police, the last man in the country who doesn't love Princess Tony.

25/1/99

Say a prayer for Harry Cogram, the Normandy veteran who hanged himself after some thoughtless town hall moron threatened to evict him for a rent debt of three pence (which he didn't even owe). The fool who wrote this letter had no idea of how shaming and hateful the idea of debt, even one so trivial, would have been to one of Mr Cogram's vintage. It was one of the many ways in which the quiet, brave, kind and patient generation now departing was better than we are.

In his last moments, did Mr Cogram wish he had died on the beaches 55 years ago, face to face with an enemy he could at least see? Or did he just wonder why he had bothered, like so many others? God rest his soul.

1/3/99

Lord Denning is one good reason why people should not abandon their accents. The great judge's Hampshire lilt lifted my heart whenever I heard it, making me think of high chalk hills and flint churches.

Listen carefully to Jim Callaghan and you will hear the soft traces of a Portsmouth burr, much loved by me because my grandfather spoke it. I don't think anyone under 50 uses it nowadays because, like so many other accents, it has been obliterated by the flat new London voice.

You have to go many miles now to find true English speech. If you are lucky enough to hear the King James Bible read by a Yorkshireman who still uses "thee" and "thou" in normal conversation, it will sound as if it was written yesterday.

Hitler ought to have known he was defeated when the wartime BBC first allowed the news to be read in a Yorkshire accent. People sometimes thought the strangled vowels of upper-class English were a sign that we were soft and effete, easy to beat. Nobody hearing the strong tones of the real Britain could ever think that.

8/3/99

In Blairland, even the storms have gone soft

The poetry of the radio shipping forecast has often been noted. That lovely phrase "falling slowly" is now the title of a novel. Nobel laureate Seamus Heaney has written verses about it. But has psychobabble crept in among these evocative, storm-tossed, rugged words? The other night, an area of high pressure was said to be "losing its identity".

You don't expect this sort of language out there in the clean, salty, wind-blasted world of Iceland and Malin Head. Has the poor thing been offered counselling? Had it been hanging around German Bight too long after losing its nerve near Rockall?

Can nothing be done?

3/5/99

Farewell to America

The train roared through the empty, haunted desert of West Texas, deer scattering away from its headlight, jagged mountains picked out by the moon, a command performance of huge stars overhead in the clear, dry air.

Nobody was looking. In the observation car, parents and children crowded round video screens watching the imaginary African veldt, in yet another re-run of Disney's overrated *The Lion King*.

Free to choose between the grandeur of their own birthright and a plastic, all-singing cartoon landscape, they picked the fake.

Is this a country disappearing up its own camera lens, so distracted by videos and the cineplex movie theatre that it no longer actually knows what it is for, or where it is?

This nation, which once formed its own view of itself in a Hollywood of stars, heroes and triumphant good, now more usually sees itself in a dark mirror where every kind of foulness is emphasised.

Is the world capital of hope and the arsenal of optimism growing old and sick? And what will happen to the rest of us if America loses its heart? As I prepare to head eastwards after two enthralling years in the USA, these and other gloomy questions seek an answer.

The temptation is to dismiss all fears, to say airily that this, the world's last great land empire, is so big, so rich and so blessed that it can withstand shocks 1,000 times as great as those which now buffet it.

I would like to think so. I have stood in various gloomy twilight outposts of the old Soviet domain and silently blessed America simply for existing. Millions of others, trapped in poverty and oppression, have made a pathetic cult of Marlboro cigarettes and Budweiser beer, clutching the packages as signs that a better world existed somewhere.

And I have resisted that stupid British snobbery which loftily dismisses the USA as a cultural desert, and mocks the clear and honest ambition of most Americans – a free, abundant life untroubled by governments and sustained by faith.

Travelling, especially away from the two coasts and their bloated, failing cities, I have almost always found civility, trust and generosity which put Britain to shame.

Even in the filth of the Robert Taylor Homes, a Chicago colony of fatherless families mired in welfare and besieged by drug gangs, where children murder children for small change, I have met mothers determined to bring up their offspring to be honest and upright.

In Washington itself, where every Sixties fad in politics, penology, sexuality and social policy is treated like holy writ, a vigorous opposition has now sprung up, speaking confidently and without embarrassment about forbidden topics such as virtue. If only fashionable London would start to debate these issues.

Of course, it is only an opposition. A president lurks in the White House who – if he believes in anything – believes in all the failed ideas which Tony Blair's Labour Party hopes to re-impose on Britain in 1997.

As if to mock Washington's marble monuments to high ideals, a convict mayor sits in the City Hall, his head lost in a cloud of bankruptcy and alleged corruption.

Each day, new horrors become apparent – abstract like the steadily growing use of narcotics by schoolchildren or all too real, like the man who cut off his son's head and hurled it from his car window on an Arizona highway.

Any journey reveals the unhealed wound of racial division – zones of doom lie on the edge of almost every major city, where jobless, hopeless (and mainly black) people roam fearfully among the broken glass.

They had no yesterday, they have no today, and they will certainly have no tomorrow.

And even in the richest suburbs, miles from the grief of the slums, teenagers slouch resentfully homewards from feeble schools to the moral poverty of empty homes. When they get there, they turn on the TV and connect their brains to a steady drip-feed of what Alexander Solzhenitsyn calls "liquid manure".

Hollywood and the music business daily continue their strangle campaign to "mainstream deviancy", making people accustomed to things which would once have horrified them. Any attack on this is dismissed as "censorship".

Official immigration policy seems designed to lure into the country anyone who cannot speak English, is unskilled and unused to the laws and customs of an advanced democracy. The people we think of as Americans, white Europeans, are expected to become the minority some time in the first half of the next century.

In great expanses of this altered cityscape, the physical and moral diseases of the Third World – tuberculosis and a triumphant drug trade – are spreading. Civilised customs are sick or dying.

While Congress postures about Bosnia – the latest moral playground for those who see foreign affairs as a way to parade their consciences – 20,000 murders are committed in the USA every year.

More and more of these slayings are carried out by strangers, erasing witnesses to lesser crimes. Like burglaries in Britain, many are insoluble, a matter for paperwork and muttered sympathy.

In the same period, police shoot 450 suspects dead while armed householders lawfully dispose of another 350 or so and criminals murder 75 cops.

In the State of Virginia, two miles from where I write this, almost any citizen now has the right to carry a hidden gun. Many ordinary but scared people are signing up for permits there and in several other states.

America's elite, quite incapable of keeping guns or syringes from city schools, has responded to this whirlpool of squalor by successfully banning prayer from every classroom in the land.

Anywhere else, it would be a picture of despair. Still, even as I pack up to leave, I continue to hope, mainly because I have to.

So much good has come out of this unique experiment that it is impossible – and frightening – to picture a world in which America has defeated itself.

3/8/95

Time travel between two worlds

This is a good place for time travel, provided you only want to go backwards. Here, where the bitter end of the old Evil Empire is just an hour's flight from the furthest outpost of the Land of the Free, they never expected normal travellers.

In fact, if I had tried the crossing five years ago, I would have been shot down by both sides.

The airspace used to hum with radar and throb with superpower tension. They ran the International Date Line down the middle of the Bering Straits, which means you can leave Russia on Monday morning and arrive in Alaska in the middle of the previous Sunday.

This is confusing, but it didn't matter until now because nobody was making the trip.

Journey in the opposite direction, and you go 60 years back in time in as many minutes: for this short stretch of icy water marks the deepest division between two human societies that ever existed. By comparison, passing through the Berlin Wall was about as dramatic as crossing the Thames.

I came out of Russia this way because I felt I could not just climb onto a plane in Moscow and be wafted out of Russian airspace, champagne in my hand. I needed to know I had crossed the frontier.

Even now, this is not a simple journey. It began with a nine-hour flight eastward from Moscow, crossing nine time zones, to the fog-shrouded town of Anadyr.

Here, Nikita Khrushchev built an underground city to house a battery of long-range nuclear missiles. Oleg Penkovsky, MI6's star spy, revealed their existence to the West.

Now that the rockets are no longer wanted, it is a half-abandoned fishing port, a weary Soviet city of cracked and listing concrete blocks, murky puddles, heaps of wreckage and old communist slogans that nobody can be bothered to take down.

"It is," they say, "your duty to toil for the Motherland." The message was probably aimed at the gulag prisoners who were forced to build the airport. It must have been a bitter thought for them that they were closer to America than they were to Moscow.

In this wasteland, I had to spend the night in a hotel like a reformatory while I waited for permission to enter the frontier zone.

As I gazed out of the dirty window into the fog, I knew that America was just beyond the horizon – but it had never seemed so far away.

Never, that is, until I got my permit and flew on to Provideniya, which is more or less the last place on earth. Set between dramatic mountains, black shale dusted with snow, this, too, was once a giant military base, the jumping-off point for a planned attack on Alaska if World War Three ever came.

At the foot of the icy mountains, Soviet power built a town so dismal I was quite scared by the thought that fog or blizzards might leave me trapped there.

Thick, crow-black smoke coils up towards the sky from filthy chimneys. Flats tremble to the endless thump and rumble of the power station.

Defeated weary figures limp and straggle along the cracked main street. Half-wild, half-breed dogs roam about, growling at the passers-by.

Once, long ago, somebody tried to brighten the prospect by painting some of the blocks of flats. It is not now clear what colour they were meant to be, but it is now a hellish mixture of orange and grey that looks rather like dried blood. Very old, dried blood.

Even more pathetic are old wall-paintings urging everyone to support perestroika (remember perestroika?). Or declaring "Provideniya – gateway to the Arctic." If the Russians had got to the moon the result would have looked something like this.

My guide through the town was the kindly but sad-faced Tolya, who had come here 20 years ago. "Do you like it here?" I asked. "No," he replied. "Then why did you come?" "I thought it would be better than where I was before. It wasn't." I didn't really need to ask him why.

Incredibly this place is now linked to Alaska by direct, if irregular, flights. A tiny customs and passport office has been opened at the little airstrip, and every few weeks a neat little Mitsubishi turbo-prop swoops down, alien as a spaceship among the Antonov biplanes and the army helicopters. To my huge relief, I had arrived on the right day. The plane was there.

Customs cleared and passport checked for the last time by Russia's relentless frontier guards, I climbed eagerly aboard and we tore along the dirt-track airstrip and lifted off, grit and debris flying up around us.

In minutes we had left Provideniya behind: suddenly it was nearly impossible to believe it was there at all. As George Orwell said of Britain's northern industrial towns in the Depression, it was "a smudge of smoke and misery hidden from us by the curve of the earth's surface".

An hour later I was in Nome, Alaska, eating prime ribsteak and drinking chilled Miller's High Life, watching baseball on the big TV in Fat Fred's Diner.

Outside, as if it was perfectly normal, were real shops, proper cars, hopeful people.

It was nothing special. Nome is an old Gold Rush town, shabby and basic by American standards, with weather-beaten streets of wooden houses.

But here people were living their lives for themselves, not directed by some vast and distant power for its own grim purposes.

I wasn't sure, and I'm still not, which of these two worlds is the real one. I have a nightmare that our little lighted circle of Western civilisation may just be an interlude between centuries of backward misery, and that Provideniya is waiting for us all if we are not very careful.

As I took the next clean, smooth Boeing southwards towards Anchorage, Seattle, Memphis and Washington, a stewardess casually placed a tray of beautiful fresh strawberries in front of me, as if there was nothing surprising about it.

Without warning, I was suddenly fighting back tears.

23/10/92

The night that free speech died

It was the night the Politically Correct mob tried to run me out of town – and very nearly succeeded. It was the night I was rescued from my foes by an incredible alliance of drug-dealer and dope advocate Howard Marks and the Blackpool Constabulary.

Late on Wednesday evening the Lancashire police actually offered to escort me from Blackpool's Winter Gardens to the railway station for the last train out. Howard Marks was at my elbow, offering protection.

But while I am grateful to Mr Marks and the police, and many other people who showed courage and democratic spirit, I now fear for free speech in this country as I never have before.

Not since I was shushed by a Czech friend on the Prague tram for talking politics in public have I seen intolerance at such close quarters.

I was in Blackpool at the invitation of the NUS to debate

the issue of cannabis legalisation with "Mr Nice", Howard Marks, the notorious drug-dealer and pro-pot campaigner. And a fine debate it was – good-humoured, fair, sometimes hilarious (Howard was smoking a very long cigarette) with an audience that peaked at around 600. There was some heckling, a welcome change in this era of ticket-only political gatherings and pre-ordained standing ovations.

Then, just as the debate was about to be thrown open to the floor, Chairwoman Julie Eason suddenly informed me that I was to be removed from the platform. I gasped with amazement, then asked her for an explanation. She said some students had objected to "offensive remarks" which I had made.

What were these remarks? She could not or would not say. She then rose to inform the audience. Most of them were as astonished as I. I tried to protest, but my microphone was pushed away and switched off.

Then the President of the NUS, Douglas Trainer, was at my side, urging me to leave and plucking at my elbow. I protested at the top of my voice that this was an outrage against free speech. At this point, to cheers, Howard Marks strode across the platform to say: "If you're going, so am I." I clasped him warmly, and arm in arm, my opponent and I left the stage.

Though I protested that I didn't need protection, a flying wedge of burly stewards insisted on guarding me through the crowd. All they were guarding me from were a few crumpled balls of paper and an excited young woman with strong opinions and a nose ring, speaking so fast that I still don't know what she was saying. Several of the audience came up to shake my hand. They said they didn't agree with me, but supported absolutely my right to speak.

How utterly unlike the sullen officials of the NUS, who refused to apologise or explain or justify what I believe was their surrender to a sort of fascist intolerance. They knew my views and my habit of stating them plainly. I was their guest. I made some forceful remarks to them at this point.

Mr Trainer eventually said he "apologised for any inconvenience caused", as if he were a delayed train rather than the president of Britain's national student body, with a stronger interest in freedom of speech than most. I urged him to arrange for the protesters to make their protest to me. He declined.

Then the police made it clear that if I did not leave, it would put them in an extremely awkward position. Unlike the NUS, they and security staff were courteous and helpful throughout.

I slipped out by a back door. A student ran up to me in the dark street. "I thought you were very badly treated," he said. "You have the right to say what you want whether we agree with you or not." He understood what the "leaders" of his union did not: that however fashionable and dominant an opinion is, it does not have the right to drive out all others.

Yesterday morning the NUS admitted they had no record of what I had said or any accurate account of it. But they read out this statement:

"The implication that Peter Hitchens was proud to be associated with sexism and homophobia was offensive to members of the audience. The NUS has an equal opportunities policy and we believe that no one should be intimidated or made to feel excluded because of their race, religion, sex, sexuality or disability. The remarks in question had caused offence and the meeting could not go on, and on the advice of the security it was necessary to remove the speaker in question."

So now I know. This is what I said: "According to your categories, I am a reactionary sexist, homophobe and an ex-Trotskyist to add to the inflammatory mixture. What is even worse, I am proud of it. If there is anyone in this hall who agrees with me, I would advise you to keep very quiet about it. You are unfashionable, the worst crime you can commit these days."

Personally, I think the words "sexist" and "homophobic" are meaningless catcalls designed to prevent any serious discussion.

They are always coupled with racialism, a disgusting prejudice which I deplore at least as deeply as anyone in the hall on Wednesday night. It is now becoming harder openly to state that you believe the sexes are different, or that you disapprove of homosexuality.

This slippery slope may end with it becoming effectively illegal to state certain views. The excuse that I was removed on "the advice of security" would be sinister if it were not pathetic.

It is the duty of those holding public meetings to ensure that free speech is protected from disorder rather than suppressed by it.

I do not believe that my NUS hosts understand this and I fear this is a sad reflection on what is now taught in our schools and universities – that the educated elite of the nation no longer has the instinct for liberty; and that was plain as a pikestaff to Howard Marks.

3/4/98

How dare they put this tax on dying?

The ever-grasping government machine can now go on thrusting its greedy, bony fist into the pockets of old people who saved for their retirement. Thanks to the Court of Appeal's decision on Friday, the foul policy of plundering the old to pay for their own care until there is almost nothing left of their lifetime savings can go on unhindered.

The Appeal Court judges overruled a colleague, who had tried to say that all nursing care was the responsibility of the NHS. What a pity.

I was telephoned recently by a lady who had been driven almost out of her mind by the prying and arrogance of the authorities when her husband fell seriously ill and needed nursing care. Strangers came and fingered through her bank statements – can you imagine this?

They cannot take their house away yet – that will come if she becomes too ill to cope – but she has been through an experience as humiliating and unjust as the hated means test of the Thirties.

It hardly needs saying that this couple both served their country with all their strength through the terrible war which our children are no longer even taught about.

This is the generation – provident, hating debt, who scrimped all their lives for the security of a house and for something to hand on to their children. They also paid their taxes and so-called "national insurance".

Now they all live in dread of the first signs of serious illness. For it will not just mean pain but the seizure of their cash and assets to pay for "care" that only a millionaire could afford. Oh, I know that it would be expensive to look after these people, as governments once promised to do.

But I can't help thinking that in all the vast and wasteful range of government spending there are plenty of things that could be cut back to stop this injustice to the old. It is a blow to the whole idea of property and inheritance, that authority should be allowed to snatch away savings and homes in this high-handed fashion.

Without the right to inherit there would be no true private property. And without private property we are all completely at the mercy of the State.

19/7/99

LORDS

Why does the Labour Party hate our constitution so much? It seems quite determined to vandalise ancient rules and institutions which have somehow kept us free for centuries, while our neighbours have groaned beneath tyrants, dictators and secret policemen.

Its latest target is the hereditary peerage. But what is wrong with inheriting things? We all hope to leave things to our children and be left things by our parents.

Inheritance is one of the most important things in life. It is a pillar of family, property and freedom.

And we do not just inherit money. It used to be a good old working-class tradition in places like the London docks that jobs were handed on from father to son.

It still goes on. One of the brightest stars in the House of Lords is Baroness Jay of Paddington, who just happens to be the daughter of Baron Callaghan, the former Prime Minister. She is also the ex-daughter-in-law of the late Lord Jay, once a Labour cabinet minister.

The truth is that Labour has no objection to inheritance as such. But it hates the independence of the hereditary peers, who cannot be bossed around by whips and spin doctors.

Britain is the one major democracy in the world whose constitution can be changed in an evening by the majority of the vote of a single chamber – a chamber more and more under the thumb of the Government.

The hereditary peers are the one part of Parliament which cannot be suborned, blackmailed or cajoled into submission by anyone.

19/1/98

Labour's plan to abolish Britain cannot succeed unless the Tory Party is first split apart and then destroyed. Tony Blair's greatest fear is that he will lose the next election and so be robbed of the chance to merge this country for ever with the European Union.

He knows that Labour governments usually do not last long, that when people realise Labour's real nature they vote them out. That is why, for the first time in modern history, a British Premier is actively working to smash the Opposition, with the cheerful help of the sheep, poodles and capons of the toadying media. If the Conservative Party dares to defend the status quo – an independent Britain under a tried and tested constitution – it will be smeared as "extremist".

The pity is that so few people in the Tory Party seem to understand what is happening. They are still behaving as if the normal give-and-take of British democracy was going on, with the two parties taking turns to bat in a national game of political cricket.

They do not see that the Government has no intention of giving up power ever; that this is not cricket but mortal combat. They have not grasped that this is a creeping, creepy putsch which will end centuries of liberty if it is not stopped.

What can Lord Cranborne have thought he was doing when he was welcomed into Mr Blair's private lair last week? In the Middle Ages, aristocrats had the doubtful privilege of being hanged with a silken rope, while the common people got plain rough hemp round their necks. Did the noble lord not see that he was being offered something just as worthless in return for going quietly to his political death?

Maybe he was too stupid to understand this but it is more likely that he believed he was saving his beloved House of Lords. That was stupid, too. Had the deal gone through, he would quickly have found out that he had not saved it. Once the mass of hereditary peers had been stripped of their votes, Mr Blair would rapidly have turned the Lords into a chamber of eunuchs.

Look what he has already done to the Commons, where robotic Labour MPs now ask "questions" written out for them by Government overseers and are not even ashamed when they are found out. William Hague was quite right to sack Lord Cranborne and behaved throughout with firmness and courage. He had been leader of the Labour Party, the press and media would have said so. Instead the baseless idea was spread about (by whom?) that his job was in danger and he was subjected to the usual insulting, partial questions from the power groupies of the State Broadcasting Service – sorry, the BBC.

If the Tories intend to fight against this attempt at dictatorship, they are going to have to understand that the Government is not an opponent: it is an enemy dedicated to their utter destruction. To bargain or compromise with it, to accept jobs or favours from it, will be fatal. Supposed concessions may be on offer, or seats on commissions, or titles, or stays of execution. They will all be tricks, like the one which Lord Cranborne fell for. If the Tories want to save the country from a dismal merger with Euroland, they must hang together from now on, despite the buckets of slime which will be chucked over them by the castrato choir of the media. Or they will all hang separately once the Dear Leader and his henchmen have won the next, crucial election.

7/12/98

Peter Hitchens is a columnist and broadcaster. He began working for *The Daily Express* in 1977 and was its correspondent in Moscow and Washington. He has witnessed the attempted 1991 Stalinist putsch in Moscow, the handshake between Yitzhak Rabin and Yasser Arafat, two executions and the launch of Britain's first Trident missile. He is married with three children and lives in Oxford.